Study Skills
for
Successful Students

Fred Orr

D1336317

ALLEN & UNWIN

To my parents

First published 1992
Allen & Unwin Pty Ltd
8 Napier Street, North Sydney, NSW 2059, Australia

National Library of Australia
Cataloguing-in-Publication entry

Orr, Fred
  Study skills for successful students
  ISBN 1 86373 118 0
  1. Study, Method of I. Title
371.302812

Typeset in 10/11 pt Times by Adtype Graphics
Printed by Loi Printing Pte Ltd, Singapore

Contents

Preface

What's this book all about? In one word: *skills*. Study skills to be more exact. They are the essential tools of trade for upper secondary and tertiary students. But, don't most students already have these skills by the time they reach upper secondary and tertiary study? Yes, the basics are generally there, but the demands of study at these higher levels will require more advanced skills.

Let me ask a few questions to see how you might assess some of your skills. Do you have high confidence in your abilities to listen effectively in class discussions and lectures? Are you able to record an accurate set of lecture notes? Can you skim through a complex chapter and get the basic messages quickly and effectively? And, looking at the end of the academic year, can you organise a thorough revision of all topics so that you enter the examination room with confidence? These questions might sound demanding, but that is exactly what studying at upper secondary and tertiary levels is all about.

These are but a few of the critical skills which many students and, indeed teachers, assume are present. However, are these skills developed and used to best advantage? Many years spent counselling secondary and tertiary students have shown me that the rudiments of the skills are there, but they certainly need to be developed further. This book will show you how to develop those skills which one day might well give you the needed leverage to gain your qualification or attain your desired job.

Given that this book is about study skills, who should read it? The book is specifically written for upper secondary and tertiary students. That means students from Year 10 onwards can profit well from reading and then *applying* the messages of this book. You will readily identify with the case studies taken from students in high school, technical college and university. Some of these students have battled through their courses to achieve very high results. Others have experienced more difficulty. The message here is that every experience has potential learning value, even the test paper or essay which is returned with a failing mark. Looking on the bright side, such a result is an invitation to sharpen one's skills, and reading this book is a very good way to go about it.

In addition to the target groups of secondary and tertiary students, three other very important groups of readers are lecturers, teachers and parents, all of whom have strong vested interests in the academic outcomes of their students and children. These individuals will find the book to be a vital academic resource. It delivers a critical set of skills to their students and children, which makes their teaching and parenting roles much easier.

Ideally, the book should be read when the serious years of studying start. Ask any group of students and they'll tell you that studying gets serious soon after Year 9. That's when they are asked to start making decisions about subjects to be studied for their future careers. Some students will turn the proverbial blind eye to these academic decisions and demands and, indeed, they might even opt out of the system. However, many return in the following years to gain the qualifications necessary to advance in their careers.

But why is studying important? Admittedly, you are not likely to be asked to recite the dagger scene from Macbeth ten years down the track, unless of course you are an actor or an English literature teacher. The essence of effective and efficient studying is not about memorising tonnes of trivial details. It *is* about developing yourself and your skills. That certificate, diploma or degree which is awarded at the end of your academic career tells a prospective employer you have the vital three D's—discipline, diligence and determination which are very valuable and marketable qualities. And, when the employment market is tight and tough, pieces of paper count—*a lot*. Your qualification will be the object of keen employer interest in the first screening process which separates the also-rans from the interviewees in the job hunt.

You now know something about the scope of this book and the audience for whom it is written. You might be interested in the best way to read the volume. From a time management perspective, start with the chapters which are likely to be of the most immediate benefit. If you have exams starting in two weeks, the chapters on revision skills and examination techniques will be the place to start. The principle is to get the most value out of the book as soon as possible.

Each chapter is prefaced by a set of points which tell you the topics covered in the chapter. Many of these points will be section headings, allowing you to identify quickly the possible places of interest. Get to the meat of the matter, apply the skills, and return to the other chapters when time permits.

In order to get maximum value from this book, try what I call the TUF approach. The letters stand for: try, use and fun. Learning any new set of skills will be significantly advanced by *trying* them *frequently*. The more you try, the more skilful you become. The *use* part of the exercise means you should use the skills in a variety of settings. If, for example, you can argue, question, discuss, or even sing, dance or dramatise Dalton's Law, then there is a very good chance you won't forget it. Sounds a bit zany, but it's true. Even a weekly lunchtime discussion group with two classmates to work through the concepts of your toughest subject will pay dividends.

The final part of the TUF approach is to try and make your learning *fun*. If you're having fun, then learning will be enjoyable and most likely easy. The ways to make your learning fun are limited only by your imagination. See if you can organise contests, games, dramas and competitions in order to master a topic. No one says that learning has to be dull and dreary. Indeed, top level executives have been introduced to games as a fun way to learn new management skills. At the student level, involve others in helping to make your learning *fun*.

At this point, it's over to you. Decide where you want to start in the book; read the chapter, and then apply the skills as soon as possible. Practice is the key to improvement.

Enjoy the book, practise the skills, prepare for success!

Fred Orr
Sydney, 1992

1
Personal management strategies

- Motivation
- Concentration
- Procrastination
- Memory enhancement

Emma was a first-year student in interior design, who had spent two years travelling and working overseas after completing her high school studies. Following this carefree existence, she had strong concerns about being able to sit down and keep her mind focused upon her studies. She liked art and design and felt reasonably committed to the three-year course during the first several weeks. However, as soon as assignments were received and exams were being mentioned, her commitment and motivation were thrown into question. She wondered whether she had just fallen out of practice of systematic and disciplined study, or whether she was frightened of failing.

The thought of generating 2000 words on the first essay caused panic in her mind and shivers in her body. She avoided the project until the last weekend and then staged a frantic work session to get something down onto paper. During that last-ditch effort, she reported her mind could not function correctly—her concentration was weak, her memory was erratic and her powers of creativity were absent.

From the above description, you can see that Emma presented a common but serious set of problems. After several counselling sessions, Emma admitted that the underlying cause of many of her problems was a lack of motivation. She just had not been able to shake the very relaxed and laissez-faire lifestyle which she had been living. Getting down to the hard work of systematic study had eluded her so far. We discussed various ways she might increase her motivation and thereby improve some of the other study problems as well.

Motivation

Just as in Emma's situation, motivation problems can be a major source of trouble for many students. If getting motivated is a problem for you, here are some practical pointers to help.

- Buy an exercise book to use as a work diary and make a daily list of your study tasks. Tick the study tasks as you accomplish them. The ticks become a record of work accomplished. Looking over the pages of ticked items will give you a positive feeling of achievement and spur you on to even more accomplishments.
- Rewarding positive action is a good motivator. Select rewards which will be personally appealing, such as going to a film when a major project has been finished. It's best not to use food as a reward, as dietitians will rightly claim that food should only be used as a source of nutrition. Make a list of other rewards which are personally appealing and use them to prompt increased motivation and enhanced productivity in your studies.

- Invite several classmates from your most difficult subject to join a lunchtime study group and meet weekly to discuss the topics raised in the last several lectures. Choose people who are serious about their study. If each person takes responsibility for preparing three questions, the lunchtime meeting can then follow a disciplined format of discussion which is mutually beneficial to all.
- Make a revision chart and post it in front of your study area. Every time you look up you will be reminded of the necessity to maintain a steady and progressive campaign of revision. Remember, regular revision is the key to exam success—and this key is best turned regularly every week. It will unlock many of the problems facing you in the exam room.
- If personal discipline is not your strongest characteristic, then consider giving a list of the goals you plan to accomplish each week to a family member or close friend. Arrange a regular weekly meeting with this person to report on your progress.
- Clarify your vocational goals. If you know where you are headed, then you are more likely to get there even if the route takes you over some rough ground. Talk to people working in the vocational area you are aiming for. Ask them about the satisfactions they derive from their work, but also take into account the dissatisfactions.
- If you are quite convinced that you want to work as a computer systems engineer, advertising copywriter, medical specialist or oriental rug dealer, for example, then make a large business card for yourself and post it where you will see it frequently. The card will remind you of your goal and spur you on to greater efforts.
- If you feel like you are burning out from too much stress and pressure, then be certain to take more frequent study breaks. Also, schedule the occasional weekend away and completely free yourself from worries about studying. Just enjoy some peaceful surroundings and perhaps the relaxing company of friends. You will return to your books with renewed vigour and drive following such an interlude.

In summary, motivation is one of the most frequent problems expressed by students. Motivating yourself is fully *your responsibility* (not the job for your teaching staff, your parents or friends). The above suggestions may help. Try them. If you make a success of today, then you have already greased the gears for a successful tomorrow. The essence is to try and try. There is absolutely no substitute for experience.

Concentration

In addition to increased motivation, just about every student would like the formula to produce more concentration.

Liz was a student in information management (library science) and she often studied in the quiet recesses of the book stacks. The problem was that the quietness of the surroundings seemed to induce daydreaming and more than occasionally, sleep. Her attempts to concentrate ended in frustration. I suggested she try the following concentration booster, the 15 x 4 technique.

This technique is really a method of studying in short bursts of fifteen minutes each. With short study bursts and frequent short breaks, your mind can maintain high concentration and continuing vigour. Here's how to apply the technique.

1 Buy yourself an exercise book for recording your study tasks.
2 At each study session, start by writing specifically what you intend to accomplish in the first fifteen minutes. Be realistic and success-oriented, so underestimate your goal rather than plan to accomplish too much. As you progress, you will become a more accurate estimator in what you can accomplish in fifteen minutes.
3 Accomplish the goal. Keep your head down and your mind glued to the task. You will probably find that any thought wandering will be checked, as even a three-minute daydream is compromising 20 per cent of your goal time.
4 Rule a column down the right side of the page for red ticks, the symbol of task accomplishment. At the end of your first fifteen-minute goal, tick the task and note the small, but pleasant feeling of accomplishment which that action produces.
5 Take a one-minute break. That's just sixty seconds, so

there's no time to ring the love of your life to discuss the day's events. Be content to move away from your desk, do some mild stretching exercises and then sit down for the next bout.

6 Repeat the above cycle four times, being certain to specify sufficiently short goals to maximise the opportunities for success, tick each task as it is accomplished and take just a sixty-second break.

When you apply this technique, you will quickly discover that it's quite intense. Your mind will be churning—no time for daydreaming! The work you get through may be surprising, but pleasing. As you will guess, such intense work will create fatigue. Following each cycle of 4 fifteen-minute work periods, take a slightly longer break, say five to ten minutes. The breaks are very important as hard work requires adequate rest.

If you're studying for long periods, as might be the case during the pre-exam 'stu vac' periods, then you will want to space these 15 x 4 cycles so that your mind can rest sufficiently between study periods. Steve, a post-graduate accountancy student, had his professional qualification exams coming up in four weeks. Even though he was working full-time for a very demanding chartered accountancy firm, he adopted what most students would see as Draconian tactics to ensure that he had enough time for revision.

Steve arrived at his office at 5.00 am. Yes, 5.00! He was there before the cleaners. He did have to arrange for special clearance from his manager so that the overnight security people would not think the building was being burgled when he arrived. He started his 15 x 4 revision cycles at 5.15 and worked through two of them until about 7.30. He then took a fifteen-minute break, returning at about 7.45 to put in another one-hour cycle before his normal work day commenced. He was astonished at the amount of work he covered in those early morning revision sessions. Obviously, no one disturbed him with phone calls and for the greater part of the time, no one else was on the floor. His exam results? An overall distinction.

You will readily admit from your past experience that efficient studying is hard work. Because we are but mere mortals, any appealing option to this hard work is very likely to break our concentration. The solution to this potential pitfall is to know your personal vulnerabilities and then take preventive action. Find a location where you will be least likely to be distracted. Think about noise, visual interference, even aromas. Many students think that the library is an ideal place for concentrating on their work, but when they get settled, they find themselves frequently looking up and around. Their eyes scan the area for anybody interesting who might provide an appealing distraction. If you fall into this category, then find a place where you can not see anyone else. As for noise and aromas, choose your study places carefully. If the TV or radio is blaring away at home, exercise your diplomatic skills and ask the viewers or listeners if they would mind turning the equipment down or perhaps using earphones.

In summary, concentration is a mental skill which can be developed with practice, much like building more muscles with daily exercise. The 15 x 4 technique will not only generate greater concentration skills, but it will also carry you through a surprising amount of work. All of the best intentions to concentrate can be destroyed by distractions. Get up early, before any potential distractors have woken up. Get to your study place and get to work. For more normal times of study, do what you can to control your study environment and then exercise firm personal discipline to get your stipulated work done.

Procrastination

Procrastination seems to be endemic on most campuses. 'Tomorrow' is the salvation for procrastinating students, as it means they can ease off, avoid or delay the preparation today. However, the todays will roll by and the threatening events, essays and exams, will come ever closer. Your anxiety progressively builds with all of the delayed preparation, thus encouraging you to procrastinate yet again. For many, the tension peaks the night before the crucial event and then it's panic stations! You will probably know the scenario from that point onwards.

Is this the recipe for punctual, high performance work? Definitely, *no*, but the pattern is surprisingly common. Perhaps the case of George will ring a few familiar bells.

George, a future barrister, was the first member of his family to go to university. His parents were both factory workers and they took great pride in telling their co-workers and members of their cultural community what a good lawyer George was going to be. They were justifiably proud of their son.

George was proud as well to be in law school, but he was aware that his admission score had been borderline. He was granted special consideration for admission on grounds of financial hardship. Because of his concessional admission, he felt that all of his classmates were much brighter than he was. He also knew that many came from families of lawyers. These thoughts tended to plague his mind so that he could not get on with his work. His essays were always late and the patience of the teaching staff was stretched to breaking point. That point was finally reached when he failed to appear for two mid-term exams. George was referred to me for counselling, as the staff realised that personal issues were inhibiting his academic potential.

George reported having an ever-present fear of failure, as he felt the pride of his family rested upon his academic results. Rather than try and possibly fail, he found reasons why he should not try each day. He preoccupied himself with fix-it jobs around the house and any other excuse he could find to avoid studying. He always thought that tomorrow would be a better, more motivating day to get back to the books.

We discussed the reasons for his procrastination problem. He was relieved to hear that he had lots of company on campus. As a result of the counselling, George decided to see his career as his own responsibility and not to feel he was the sole support of his family's pride. From a practical standpoint, he started planning ahead by setting weekly and daily goals and prepared daily for classes. The results were very positive. Here are some practical pointers for procrastinating people.

- Try to determine why you have been procrastinating: fear of failure? fear of criticism? self-demands for perfect work?
- If the reasons for your procrastinating habits elude you, then talk with a counsellor. An objective view from outside will help.
- Plan each day and write down your tasks to be accomplished in a diary. Tick the tasks as you accomplish them.

- For an additional prompt, give a list of your goals to a close friend and meet several times a week to discuss the progress you are making.
- If perfectionism is a problem, try to adopt what I call an 'acceptable level of approximation'. That is, you prepare your work to a level acceptable to you, but short of the perfect point, and then hand it in. Waiting until perfection is reached can be a very long wait.
- Break large and intimidating jobs down into small achievable bits and work diligently at these bits. Tick the small jobs as you go to provide the reinforcement and assurance that progress is being made.
- Make a wall chart of study tasks accomplished. Seeing visual evidence each day of positive progress will help to keep your momentum going.
- Ask yourself frequently each day what is the most important mark-earning job which you should be doing right now. That question will induce you to consider essay preparation tasks and exam revision.
- To cope with the temptation to do 'busy work' jobs which can draw you away from your studies, make a list of other jobs to do. Look for an opportunity when they can be done in a concentrated manner, preferably at a time which will not detract from your academic work.
- Try to make daily studying a productive habit. Get to your study place at the same time each day and get straight to work. Start with an easy task to gain momentum.
- Prior to taking study breaks, which are important to keep your mind fresh and alert, write down the time of your return to study and note the task to be done. Planning ahead, even in this short span, will help you to keep focused and to keep going.

Putting these pointers into practice will help even the most diehard procrastinator to get moving on their *relevant academic work*. If difficulties arise, be certain to discuss your situation with a counsellor. Changing behaviour patterns is hard work. Some assistance from an experienced helper will make the job easier.

Memory enhancement

There are three situations in which students will complain of faulty and/or insufficient memory: when reading texts, while listening in class, and when revising for exams. Let's look at each in turn.

Remembering what you read

How often have you finished reading a section of a text and realised that you have little if any recall of the subject matter? More often than you would like to admit, I'm sure. Remembering what you read, especially if the material is difficult, is hard work. Your mind will have to be thinking, questioning, associating and generally processing the information as you proceed. Sounds exhausting, doesn't it?

While remembering what you read should not necessarily be exhausting, you should, however, be prepared to work. The chapter on reading skills describes the SQ3R technique: *survey, question, read, recite, recall.* The surveying and questioning are done as a warm-up before you actually start reading the material. As you progress, pause and recite the major points from each section. Link these points to the prime topics in the subsequent sections. This reading technique will enhance your memory for what is being read, but it will take more time than the standard 'get to it, dash through it' approach which leaves most students with only fuzzy recall.

Even if you apply the SQ3R technique assiduously, you may still find that your recall fades over the following several days. That's perfectly normal, as your mind experiences an 80 per cent decay in short-term memory within 24 hours. In order to retard this decay process, you will need to revise the major points gleaned from your reading. Try to revise the chapter by running your eyes over the underlined or highlighted phrases once or twice over the next several days. These revisions need not take very much time, perhaps just five or ten minutes, but that small investment of time will be well rewarded. To prove it, try it. You'll be surprised at how much you retain after several revisions.

Remembering what is said in class

The same principles which operate in recalling what you read are applicable to recalling what is said during lectures and other classes. Remembering is a higher mental function and best achieved when the mind is warmed up to the task. As is described in the chapter on listening and note-taking, be certain to warm up for classes by browsing through the relevant chapter or references. That warm-up need only take about five minutes. While browsing, look for section headings and major topics in **bold-face** print. Read captions of graphs and charts. When mentally noting these topics, ask yourself what does *that* mean. How does it relate to the overall concept being presented? What relationship does it have to the previous topic(s)? These are just a sample of possible questions you might ask. Questions will hook your mind and perhaps grab your interest. When the topics are mentioned later in class, you will experience an 'Ah-hah! There it is!' response which will enhance your memory for the items. The essence of this technique is warming up before class. Preparation is powerful.

Remembering what you revise

Most students hate revision. It's hard work and the whole process is intimately connected to the anxiety-producing experience of exams. For that reason, revision is generally shelved until the very last minute. Folders of notes are opened the night or two before exams, leaving only a small amount of time to cover a very substantial amount of work. These last-ditch efforts are too late for most students. However, there are always tales of exceptional efforts made during the early morning hours by extraordinary students who win high marks. These are tales and they are not always supported by hard facts.

You might have already guessed the message—you need considerable time and lots of effort to prepare thoroughly for your exams. Two nights of revision, even if they are all-nighters, will not be sufficient for most students. The best approach is to start your revision in the first weekend of the semester and learn your class notes from the first week. Use these learned concepts over the following week and then repeat the process the next weekend. Learning and then using the concepts will increase your memory and facilitate understanding. Remember, *information revised and used is information retained.*

Revision/Memory practical pointers

- Learn as you go. Revise each weekend for the semester exams.
- Use the information you are learning: debate, question, argue, present, criticise—even sing or dance to it if you can.
- Revise your notes at least five times, focusing at first on retaining the major concepts, then proceeding to subtopics, subsectional headings and finally to supporting details.
- Use coloured pens, highlighters, arrows, asterisks and any other visual aid which will help you to recall concepts in your notes.
- Be wary about recopying large sections of notes. Writing is a very time-consuming process and you are likely to gain more from several readings of the notes in the same time it would take to rewrite a section or two.
- If your mind recalls easily geometric designs, try to arrange your concepts to be learned as pyramids, squares, circular patterns or any other shape which will facilitate your recall. Recalling one element of the design is then likely to suggest the next part.
- Acronyms are handy. Make a word out of the first letters of the items to be learned. Is anyone in doubt about the meanings of radar and scuba? These words are now part of our language, but initially they meant 'radio detection and ranging' and 'self-contained underwater breathing apparatus'.
- Mnemonics are the next step after acronyms. (But, remembering how to spell 'mnemonics' is a first-order challenge!) Mnemonics are rhymes or sayings constructed from words starting with the first letters of the terms you want to remember. Most medical students will know this memory aid for the cranial nerves: On Old Olympus' Towering Top, A Fat-Assed Garbageman Viewed Some Hops. The rhyme

is easily remembered and it prompts the doctors to be able to recall the names of the nerves beginning with the capitalised letters.

- Use any sense, smell, touch, taste, sound, sight, which is likely to help your memory. Who hasn't recalled a particular experience from their earlier years when they hear a song from the past? What about a smell or aroma? Freshly mown grass? A favourite perfume? These sensory experiences facilitate recall. See if there are any possible uses in helping to recall your concepts.

Practical exercises

Motivators

People are some of your best motivators. Make a list of the tasks you want to accomplish by the end of next week. Give a copy of the list to a family member or friend and arrange a meeting with this person soon after the end of the week to report on your progress.

Or make a large business card with your name, your future profession, your qualifications and any other information which you would like to include. Post the card in front of your desk so that you see it every time you lift your head. The card will remind you where your present studies are leading you.

Concentration enhancer

Practise the 15 × 4 method described in this chapter. Work in short bursts, but take frequent breaks between tasks. Your mind will stay fresh while you progress rapidly and effectively through your work.

Procrastination preventer

As with the motivation method mentioned above, giving a family member or friend the list of the tasks you intend to accomplish in the next week will prompt more personal action. Just writing a list on your own allows you to rationalise and avoid.

Memory improver

As discussed in this chapter, memory is a function of repetition and application. The more you run the information through your mind, the greater your recall. Using the information in discussions or in any practical way will help you to recall the information more easily. Make flash cards connected in the upper left corner by string and place crucial terms on one side and their definition or associated facts on the other. Carry a bundle of these cards with you each day and resolve to go through the entire bundle at least three times during the day.

2
Time and stress management

- The daily To Do list
- The semester plan
- Long-term career goals
- Preventing time robberies
- Study stress
- Sharing resources
- Diet
- Sleep
- Physical exercise

Paula and Jim were sister and brother and both were students. Paula was a first-year university drama student and Jim was finishing his matriculation studies and hoping to gain entry to architecture. Jim was thought by his high school teachers to be a student with high potential, but his marks were only in the high average range. Paula's results were somewhat better. She had always been hard working, because she felt that learning wasn't easy for her.

Jim was asked by his parents to see me because he seemed never to reach his potential. During the initial interview, Jim mentioned that his sister, Paula, always seemed to get better marks. He said she was a hard worker and also that she seemed to be much better organised. During the time I worked with Jim, it became very clear that he lacked this organised approach. He pursued his studies in a helter-skelter fashion with absolutely no overall plan. He meandered through his days like a pinball, being bounced off one obstacle to another. His study priorities, whenever he paused to consider them, were mostly determined by panic.

As a result of working with Jim, I met Paula who occasionally suffered from almost the opposite problem—she pushed herself almost to the point of a breakdown. She was very organised and determined, but rarely took breaks and sometimes worked through entire weekends without seeing or ringing her friends. Towards the end of the year, she was visibly stressed and feeling lethargic. She had dark circles under her eyes, was chronically tired, losing weight, and sleeping at every opportunity, including during classes.

The two scenarios represented by Paula and Jim demonstrate the difficulties which can arise from time mismanagement on the one hand and too much stress on the other. This chapter will address both situations, dealing first with efficient time management and then effective stress prevention. As you will see, the two are often closely related.

The daily To Do list

For most students, your course will entail too much work and your days will offer too little time. Your options to cope with this dilemma seem to be: make your days longer; lighten your study load; or, become more efficient. The last option seems to be the preferred one.

Increasing your efficiency is really a function of getting as much as possible done in the available time. Ask any really busy person how they manage their time and just about every one of these individuals will say they use some sort of list. The busier you get, the more important it is to write things down. The best way to handle a long and sometimes complex array of study tasks is to simply write them down and then decide where you will start. Here's one way you might try to organise your days.

Buy an exercise book or some other diary type notebook which is rugged enough to sustain the wear and tear of student life. Use a new page for each day and write four column headings at the top of the page: *Task, Priority, Time, Done.*

Under the task column, list every job which is currently needing attention. This will include homework assignments which are due tomorrow as well as longer term projects due in four to six weeks. You can also include personal chores, domestic duties or any other tasks which need to be done that day. When noting these tasks, be certain to be specific. For example, it is just too general to say 'Do a bit of history.' If you have just opened your history book and your best friend rings to invite you over to see a video, you might say to yourself, 'Yes, I've done a bit of history! To the video.' It would be far better to specify, 'Read pages 126–138, history; do review quest's 1–6 end of chapter.' That is a much more specifically stated task for planning purposes.

The priority column is fairly straightforward. After listing all the tasks, read through them and assign a 1, 2 or 3, depending upon how important and urgent they are. The number one jobs, those that are both important and urgent, need attention today and should be done first. The number two jobs are less urgent and may be carried over until tomorrow, if time is tight. The number three jobs are least urgent and least important and you may even find that they don't get done at all after being carried forward over several days. Be sure to focus on the number one category, as this is generally going to include mark-earning study jobs—preparation of essays and reports and revision for exams. When in doubt about study tasks, get to those jobs which are going to earn you marks.

The time column is simply your estimate of how much time you think the various tasks might take. By estimating the respective times for various tasks, you can prevent the frustrating experience of planning a day's work and then finding that you really need a week to accomplish all of the tasks. For example, there's really no sense in listing on your daily plan, 'Read *War and Peace*', as most students will require weeks to work their way through this colossal tome.

The done column is reserved for ticks which you record after completing the individual tasks. Be certain to include this column and to use it, as it represents a reward after working through your task. Giving yourself a tick upon task completion might seem juvenile to some, but consider the following. Carpenters, painters and other tradespeople produce tangible and visible results after a day's work. Students, on the other hand, frequently miss out on this very positive experience. After reading a textbook for several hours, you might feel exhausted and drained. Yes, you have worked very hard at your reading and you think you understood the work, but is there anything to show for all of this hard labour? Generally, no. However, if you have been ticking off reading goals by sections, then at least you will have some evidence of work completed. A series of ticks can hold a surprising amount of reward value. Who doesn't like to feel that surge of fulfilment on ticking off a job as completed? I'm sure you do.

Thus, the daily To Do list is a very efficient and functional way of organising your days. If you make positive and productive use of today by organising your tasks and your time, then you will have generated considerable momentum for tomorrow. After several days of efficient and productive work, you will feel great just paging through your study diary and seeing all of those ticks in the *Done* columns. Assuming you have focused upon the number one jobs first, you will experience a major longer term benefit as well—higher marks. How can you possibly lose with such a system?

The semester plan

Having started by organising your days, you will realise how important it is to look ahead several weeks to plan for the larger projects. The best approach to take is to construct a semester plan.

Cut a Manila folder in half along the seam and holding it horizontally, rule one page in the following manner. You will be drawing columns and rows to construct a grid, so that your assignments and exams can be inserted into a box opposite the subject and under the correct week of the semester. Draw a column for your subjects down the left border. Across the top, draw a sufficient number of columns for the total number of weeks in the semester, plus several for the examination period as well. Draw in the row lines across the page so that each subject you are presently studying is represented down the left-hand border of the chart. The sample chart below shows how the system works.

Semester-at-a-Glance Chart

	Weeks													
	1	2	3	4	5	6	7	8	9	10	11	12	13	14
Maths					Ass.					Ass.				Exam
Hist.				Rpt.		Tst.		Rpt.				Prj.		Exam
Econ.				Ess.						Ess.				Exam
Phil.							Tst.					Prj.		Exam

Key: Tst = test   Ass = assignment
Rpt = report Prj = project

You will note in the chart that a variety of different assessable tasks have been written in the boxes opposite a particular subject and under a specific week. At one glance, you can see exactly where your very heavy periods are going to be. Another important feature of the semester plan is that dotted lines have been inserted from a preceding week and lead up to a report, essay, project or an exam. The dotted lines represent lead-up time, or the period over which you want to be actively working on each task.

As assignments are given to you, simply note the task in the relevant box and draw a lead-up arrow to indicate the preparation time. Generally speaking, the first day of preparation time for any assignment is the day it is assigned. If you are given three or four major essays or projects at the beginning of the semester, decide how many weeks you plan to spend preparing each one and insert the dotted arrow on your semester plan.

To make best use of the semester plan, either carry it with you in a notebook or post it on the wall directly in front of your study place. Whenever you look up from your books, the overall agenda for the semester will be clearly apparent. That image of work to be done should act as a strong motivator as well as a systematic organiser.

When writing your daily To Do list, consider the tasks which are due for submission over the next four to six weeks and include the relevant weekly sub-goals in your list. Refer to Chapter 7 for further information on planning your major projects.

The last entry for most of your subjects on the semester plan will be your exam. Final exam preparation is often neglected or vigorously repressed by most students during the early weeks of the semester. Few want to start revising for their exams following Week One, but that is the best time to start. Remember, exams will count for a very large percentage of your final marks in most subjects. Therefore, get started early on your revision and learn as you go. Draw lead-up arrows from Week One of the semester all the way through the weeks and terminating at the exam for each subject. Those dotted arrows will remind you that ongoing revision is important, indeed necessary, if high marks are to be achieved.

Long-term career goals

Having described how to organise your days and plan your semesters, let's turn now to career goals. At present, you might not know what you want to do as a career, and generally, that is OK. You might say that you feel frustrated trying to get on with your studies when you really aren't certain where these studies will take you. Yes, it is difficult trudging ahead in an apparent fog, hoping that your steps will lead you to some worthwhile destination. But, if stopping and standing still is your only option, that won't help your plight. Generally, moving ahead is far preferable to standing still, as experience will teach you something, even if it makes you decide to change paths and head off in a different direction.

Knowing where you are going is definitely a help in mapping your way and moving your feet. People with specific, set goals are more likely to get to their destinations. But, what can you do to clarify your career goals? Here are some pointers.

- Consult a careers advisor at school or in your community. Let the advisor get to know you—your interests, talents and skills as well as your dislikes and personal weaknesses.
- Visit career centres and libraries to read relevant reference materials.
- Take advantage of work experience programs which give you some first-hand experience in a workplace.
- Arrange to see several people who are working in a job area which you find interesting. The following questions will help you to understand the jobs which they do: What satisfactions do you gain from your job? What dissatisfactions are involved? What are the career prospects in the job area? If you were to start your career again, what changes would you make? Take notes and compare the replies. Discuss your conclusions with a careers advisor or counsellor.
- If you have absolutely no idea what career you wish to pursue, make an appointment to see a psychologist for career interest and aptitude testing.
- Be prepared to change your career goals as you acquire more experience. Many individuals change careers several times and do not really get settled into a long-term career until they are well into their twenties or even their thirties.
- For adults, returning to study at a mature age can possibly open up some new career goals. For example, mothers who seek an educational qualification after raising a family might well benefit from speaking with other women who have faced the same dilemma. It is important to understand and anticipate possible uncertainties and feelings of inadequacies. Contact with other mature age students will

help you appreciate that your past experiences are much more worthwhile than you probably realise. Additionally, you might discover you have a talent or skill which could blossom into a career. Once again, seek professional assistance from a careers advisor or counsellor if perplexed. Don't expect to have all the answers simply because of your age.

Preventing time robberies

Time will be one of your most scarce, but important resources as a student. The days and weeks will fly by and before you know it, you will be sitting on the doorstep of the examination room, and one hopes feeling confident. As time is almost as important as money, (some management experts say, 'Time *is* money.'), it is vital for you to prevent time robberies. The robberies, by the way, are generally *self-induced*. Here are some pointers about how to protect your time.

Television and radio

Students often say that they simply can not survive long study sessions unless they have the occasional 'hit' of TV. Alternatively, some have the radio blaring loudly to move them rhythmically along in their work. Some helpful hints about these electronic marvels:

- Plan your TV viewing, if it is necessary at all. Set the oven timer for thirty minutes and when the signal goes off, get back to your books.
- Consider standing up when you watch TV. It's much easier to move away from the set when the program is over.
- Tell a family member or flatmate what you intend to watch and at what time you plan to return to your studies.
- If you live alone or with other TV addicts who really can not afford television time, then seriously consider moving the set to the least comfortable place in the house (the garage?) or, better yet, sell the set, give it away, or ceremoniously put a brick through it (turn the power off first!).

Time-robbing visitors

When people come to visit, even if it's just crouching by your desk in the library where you're trying to study, they can rob you of valuable study time. Studies have shown that in the business sector, colleagues who drop by to visit a workmate will stay for an average of seventeen minutes. Several visits a day can certainly drain the productivity potential of the organisation. How do you protect your study time from these visitors? Try the following:

- Post a Do Not Disturb sign on your door, if you have a door to your study area. Better still, lock the door.
- If a visitor invades your study area, stand up immediately. Do *not* offer the visitor a chair. Walk the visitor away from your desk and agree on a mutually convenient meeting time, if a meeting is necessary.
- Keep any chairs near your study area stacked high with computer print-outs and heavy reference books. Visitors will have no option but to stand, and standing conversations take far less time than those conducted while sitting.
- A terrorist tactic—hang your unwashed squash clothes, suitably incubated in a warm cupboard in an airtight plastic bag, over the chair next to your desk prior to the visit of any regular visitor whom you are trying to discourage.
- Be assertive. Just tell any visitor that you're busy. Arrange a mutually suitable time to meet if you want to discuss something.

In summary, managing your time is a skill which can be developed with practice. The student who conquers the clock is at a considerable advantage. Students who continue to suffer defeats are academically at risk.

Study stress

Over recent years, people have been 'suffering from stress', have 'stressed out', and have pursued courses on 'stress management'. Stress, as the saying goes, seems to be the psychological flavour of the month or year. Looking at stress objectively, it can be fairly stated that if you are not stressed in some form, you are probably dead. While that might seem morbid, it does imply that some forms of stress can be positive. Would you not feel excited, or positive stress, at receiving a mark of 95 per cent on a difficult exam? Thus, stress can affect students both positively and negatively. When circumstances push the demand levels to the extremes, we call the condition study stress.

Barbara was the second eldest of four girls in a single parent family. Her mother worked very long hours to ensure that her daughters had all the benefits of education, plus music lessons, gym group, ballet and netball. All four girls felt they owed their mother a lot and wanted to excel in what they did.

During the high school years, Barbara worked very long hours at her studies and carried two part-time jobs to help out financially. She was able to sustain this heavy workload without too much strain, but when she entered university, the pressure became more intense. Reading time was tripled and her assignments involved much more work. She cut down on her sleep to five or six hours to achieve more study time and drank about seven cups of coffee a day to stay alert. She frequently missed meals. Weekends were spent behind her desk working through a mountain of books. She became more remote and close friends rarely saw her out of class time. Her mother became concerned when an aunt visited and remarked at how drawn and worn-out Barbara looked.

While Barbara thought her mother was just being overly concerned, she did agree to see a counsellor to discuss how things were going. When Barbara described her workload and how she was coping with it, she tried to be strong, but her eyes became glassy and soon teary. After a good cry, she admitted that she was worn to a frazzle and felt that her life had become a relentless battle against the clock and the curriculum. She was pursuing high marks, but she felt as if failure was chasing her and biting at her ankles. She feared she might fail and disappoint her mother and set a bad example for her sisters. We discussed ways in which she might cope better with the workload and return to a more effective and enjoyable lifestyle.

One of the problems which Barbara described was that she faced the growing mountain of work alone. Similarly, most of the work you will be asked to do will be solitary study, but there will be opportunities to work together with other classmates. In some subjects, you may be assigned to work in a student syndi-cate. Generally, these are both productive and enjoyable experi-ences. However, co-operative learning need not be limited to study syndicates.

Why not work with a classmate in your most difficult subject? Michael, a technical college student in engineering mechanics, found coping with his course to be difficult. During a casual conversation with a classmate, they both realised that they were struggling to keep pace. However, they found their discussion of some of the class topics to be very helpful. As a result of this casual meeting, they decided to meet each Thursday throughout the semester to discuss class topics over lunch. Their meetings were so productive that they continued into the pre-exam period and met more frequently for revision sessions. Each prepared one page summaries of specified topics and gave a copy of the summaries to the other. By sharing the revision load, they both profited in two ways: they experienced less revision stress; and they gained more thorough knowledge of the study materials by exchanging ideas. As the saying goes, two heads are better than one.

Sharing the study load can be achieved in several different ways. The first step, of course, is to find one or two classmates with whom you can divide up some of the study tasks. Look for people who seem to share a keen interest in performing well. In addition to looking for individuals who are diligent and deter-mined, you want to find people who are fun to work with. A bit of laughter and good cheer can make the dreariest of tasks more tolerable. When you have found one or two willing colleagues, consider the tasks mentioned below and see if they can be shared.

- Library research—divide up the references to be found and photocopy summaries for the team members.
- Lecture notes—when time is tight, split duties and have one person attend the lecture while the others do related jobs.
- Reference reading for classes and labs—delegate readings to group members and photocopy summaries for distribution.
- Closed reserve library readings—one person do the read-ings and distribute notes to others.

- Weekly meetings—to discuss the salient issues raised in the lecture over the preceding week.
- Combined revision—meet in the pre-exam period to work through distributed summaries of highly examinable concepts and topics.

Thus, there are many opportunities for co-operative sharing of resources in your study pursuits. You will gain qualitatively from the many minds approach and quantitatively from considerable savings in time and energy.

Diet

'What we eat is what we are' is a familiar saying which probably stretches the truth somewhat. However, the role of diet in stress management is very important.

As in the case of Barbara presented above, copious cups of coffee during the long night-time study sessions would certainly have a negative effect upon her sleep. But coffee is only one potential concern when stress, studying, and diet are considered. Here are some pointers as to how you can manage your diet and minimise stress.

- Eat well-balanced meals at regular intervals.
- Care with caffeine—more than three cups a day may cause stress responses.
- Medications can be overdone—consult your doctor if you have any questions about the strength and/or duration of the prescribed medication.
- At times of high stress, such as at exam time, students can frequently eat too much or skip meals. Be particularly careful about your diet at these times.

If eating problems have been a concern for you, then see a helping professional. Problems such as anorexia and bulimia have become increasingly common, especially amongst young people. If your concern is more diet centred, then a nutritionist, dietitian or your doctor may be able to help with information and suggestions.

Sleep

Most students feel that their sleep time is constantly under assault. For many, as the study load increases, sleep time decreases. But of course there is a limit to how much we can cut into our sleep time.

How much sleep do you need to function both comfortably and competently? The answer depends upon you. Statistically, seven and three-quarter hours is the average amount of sleep which research subjects have reported they need. However, the variation is considerable, ranging from three to eleven hours.

No matter how much sleep you may need at night, if that rest time gets reduced by your heavy work load, try supplementing your night-time sleep with several short catnaps during the day. Most busy people have discovered this secret and depend upon getting several brief rest periods during each day. I generally take a ten to fifteen minute nap after lunch and perhaps another short nap either before or after dinner. That means the five or six hours of night-time sleep is increased during the day, at periods in the day when a brief rest is particularly helpful.

You might want to try the relaxation exercise described in Chapter 9 if you experience any difficulty in just shutting out the pressing matters of your day from your mind. The relaxation exercise simply focuses your mind upon a series of relaxing steps, thus preventing your mind from floating off onto some arousing or concerning issue. Try it and you will be both pleased and surprised at how rested and relaxed you can become with a bit of practice.

If getting to sleep is a problem, try counting from 100 backwards when you inhale (one number per breath in) and say 'R-e-l-a-x-x-x' as you breathe out. Visualise the numbers being drawn in your mind as you say them to yourself. You will probably not get beyond 75 in the series before you have encouraged yourself to sleep.

Physical exercise

One of the best ways of getting rid of tension is to work it out of your body with regular exercise. You do not need to work your body into a profuse sweat. In fact, just walking at a brisk pace for 30 consecutive minutes three to five times a week has been found to be a very beneficial and therapeutic form of exercise. If you can arrange for some variety and fun in the exercise program, so much the better. Consult an exercise training specialist at your local gym for detailed advice. Whatever form of exercise you do, be certain to warm up thoroughly beforehand and allow sufficient cooling down exercise afterwards. You can supplement any gym-based exercise program by looking for opportunities each day to climb stairs and walk or ride a bike instead of travelling by car, bus, or train. Your goal is to promote good physical fitness in your body and at the same time burn off any accrued psychological tensions.

In summary, managing your time and dealing with stress are very important goals for serious students. Be sure to plan your time and to get to the high priority jobs each day. Know your time robbers and take preventive action. For the stress effects, review your diet, sleep and exercise patterns and make any adjustments which you or a stress management consultant might suggest.

Practical exercises

1   Buy an exercise book and rule off fourteen pages with columns for Tasks, Priority, Time and Done. Plan your days daily and list the tasks, priorities and time estimates for completion for a two-week period. Assess your personal efficiency at the end of that daily planning period.
2   Construct a semester plan wall chart and record all mark-earning assignments. Use dotted arrow lead-up times to indicate weekly goals during the preparation period.
3   Establish a career ideas file. Cut out articles on interesting careers and follow up any serious possibilities with further reading and interviews with people who perform the same type of job.
4   If your diet and sleep are of concern, keep a diary of your meals and snacks and, as well, a note of your sleep times. Discuss your diary notes with your doctor or another relevant helping professional.

5 Discuss your fitness level with an exercise/training consultant at your local gym or health centre. Develop a weekly
program for improving your fitness and have a follow-up
assessment in six months.

3
Listening skills in lectures

'EXCUSE ME...
.. BUT CRESMOND'S
HOGGING ALL THE
SOUND WAVES SIR.'

- Listening vs hearing
- A prepared mind can listen better
- Practical pointers
- Training exercises to enhance listening skills

A crucial question: Are you a good listener? You will probably say without hesitation, Yes! But, let me now ask how many times have you found yourself sitting in class supposedly listening, and when questioned, you realise you've been fogbound. Many times, I'm sure. Unfortunately, there is a major difference between just hearing and *active* listening. If you want to become a more active listener—and win more marks—then read on.

A short case study might help to illustrate the difference between active listening and just passively existing in class. John, a first-year university engineering student, came to see me about his very poor results after first semester. He took pride in saying that he never missed one class. However, his class notes suggested that the frequency of class attendance was not related to the quality of classroom learning. His notes were sparse, messy and at best, marginally legible. He freely admitted that he counted on adding to his class notes during the pre-exam period, but time ran out.

John, like many students, thought classroom presence equaled constructive listening. Not so! Listening is a skill which most of us take for granted. Look around any classroom or lecture hall and you will see some students sitting with their chins propped up with cupped hands and with their glazed eyes staring into space. The current pages of their notebooks are generally either glistening white and note free or marked with just the occasional scribble to prove that they were there. The doodlers have created some zany masterpieces; and the dozers? Their notes resemble trails of drunken worms. Any serious survey of students supposedly listening in class will produce data of warm bodies but cold minds. Generally, the listening process for most students is less than efficient.

Susan, a final-year high school student, reported that she was anxious about her exams which were due to start in three weeks. She said her revision was progressing well, although she had just started going through her class notes. I asked to have a look at them and she produced a disorganised mess of scratch and scribble. She had legitimate cause to be worried.

Susan remarked that she missed 'a few' classes and, as she normally had difficulty getting out of bed in the morning, she often arrived late. She said many of her subjects were not very exciting or stimulating and that she often daydreamed in classes, thus missing many of the points.

As you have probably deduced, both John and Susan have presented a range of difficulties, one of which was poor listening skills. While both individuals wanted to succeed, they both appeared to be oblivious to the importance of active and accurate listening. How can you become a more effective listener? Firstly, know the difference between listening, really listening, and just hearing.

Listening vs hearing

Let me mention briefly what hearing is as opposed to active listening. Most of us have the potential to hear. We receive sound waves through our ears which transmit them through the hearing mechanism. The sound vibrations are converted to impulses which are then sent to the brain for interpretation. It's in the latter stages that hearing and listening differ. While hearing can be a passive process (has a parent or teacher ever exclaimed to you, 'Are you deaf!'), effective listening involves considerable brain activity. It's a very complex and quite delicate process, but for most of us, the system has the potential to work quite well. The emphasis is on the word, *work*.

With reference to John, he mentioned that listening was no problem as long as the lecturers and the topics were interesting. However, his daydreams frequently scored higher marks on the interest scale. He sat in the lecture hall letting the words and ideas float over his head while he was focusing upon surfing, his girlfriend, last weekend's party or next weekend's plans. Yes, his brain was involved marginally during the lecture. He was probably just hearing the words being presented, but his mind was not actively *working* upon them. The work in this case would be interpreting, analysing, classifying and carrying out other relevant cognitive functions. John needed to do much more work during lectures, especially listening accurately and attentively to the lecturer's words and thoughts.

If you're serious about your studying, then you will want to listen in class for the words relating to central ideas and concepts. Words are just acoustic symbols which represent ideas. To make any sense out of these symbols, your mind has to be very actively involved. The involvement, by the way, is best done in an undivided fashion. For example, John would be strongly advised to focus upon the engineering principles during lectures and actively exclude thoughts of last weekend's party. Easily said, but not so easy to do, as John found out.

The secret to effective listening can be wrapped up in two four-letter words, *hard work*. I wish I could replace 'hard' with 'easy', but regrettably, that's just not the case. Effective listening *is* hard work. In fact, as a student, you might expect to work harder at listening during a lecture than the lecturer is at presenting the ideas. We expect lecturers to know what they're talking about. Students, however, are generally considered to be less knowledgeable about the lecture topics. They are expected to listen, to write their lecture notes, and then to learn the presented concepts, a much more difficult series of tasks. So, it is hard work. How, then, can you make this important listening skill easier to acquire?

Pre-lecture preparation for active listening

The process of active listening in a lecture should actually start *before* the lecture. That might sound strange, but that's certainly the case. Prior to the lecture, warm up your mind for active listening. It's much like priming a pump. The priming process allows the ongoing pumping action to occur more efficiently. The same applies to warming up your body muscles for a bout of strenuous exercise. Your mind is no different. It will function better if it's warmed up for the task.

To carry out the mental warm-up, consult your course syllabus weekly to note the topics which will be the focus of the week's lectures. If you don't have a syllabus, ask the teaching staff for one. Having noted the topic(s) for the next lecture, consult your text or a reference source and browse through the relevant chapter. Browsing means paging through the chapter in about five to ten minutes. You will not be expecting solid learning to occur from such a cursory treatment. However, you should be noting the terms in **bold face** or *italics*, the section headings, the charts and graphs and any other features which the editors have designed to jump off the page at you.

When browsing through the reference chapter, your mind should be *very* active. Ask yourself the following questions. What does this term mean? How is it related to the other terms being presented in the chapter? What association does this concept have to the next? What is this graph saying to me? All of those questions might seem intimidating, but all are not likely to be immediately relevant. Once again, your mission in browsing is to warm up your mind. You want to become familiar with the topics, not to know them thoroughly at this stage.

Pam, a social work student, agreed with the recommendation that pre-reading or browsing would be helpful. However, she said she simply did not have time to spend an additional five or ten minutes per subject per day on this process. I appreciate the basic dilemma of most students—you have too much work to do and not sufficient time to do it in. However, a critical scrutiny of your daily commitments and movements will probably produce some small patches of time when this pre-reading can be squeezed in. For example, just a few minutes browsing at the bus stop or railway station in the morning might be sufficient for one or two of your classes that day. The important point to remember is that you are simply browsing to familiarise yourself with the main ideas—you are not trying to learn the material in a definitive fashion. A few minutes per subject is all that you will need to carry out this important function.

Having browsed through the reference sources, your mind will then be familiar with the terms and concepts to be presented later that day. When the principal terms and concepts are introduced in your lectures, your response will be recognition— 'Ah-hah! There it is!' It's much the same as seeing the face of a person you met briefly yesterday as the individual approaches you in a crowd. That recognition experience has a far greater impact upon you than the mass of unfamiliar faces of total strangers. Recognising the concepts and terms will give you a distinct advantage over your classmates who are generally approaching the lecture mentally cold. While they are frantic and frazzled trying to decide whether a particular term is sufficiently important to note, you are calmly getting on with the job.

Even with the best preparation for your lectures, some students can still have difficulty listening accurately because of distractions generated by other students. Imagine this scenario: you have arrived early for your class and you are paging through your text to get prepared for the lecture. The seats just behind you are taken by a group of three students intent on solving a heart-throbbing romantic problem. The passion is so great that their conversation almost drowns out the lecturer at the start of the lecture. You are stuck between the two sound sources and your listening is certainly divided and suffering. You have two options. One, turn and tell the group to be quiet. Two, move to another seat where you can listen intently. If you decide not to move during that class, then in subsequent classes, choose another seat. You will probably discover that the noisy students will return to their former seats as if drawn there by some territorial homing instinct. You can sit at an acoustically comfortable distance and concentrate on the lecture.

If you have to select a seat where your listening will be optimised, where should you sit? Studies have shown that students sitting in the front rows of classrooms and lecture theatres do better academically. Why is this? A reasonable explanation might be that students sitting very close to the lecturer are going to feel conspicuous and easily identified should they show signs of poor attention or impending sleep. They will also be less likely to talk to other students, read the newspaper or carry on in any other irresponsible way. Additionally, by sitting close to the lecturer, you will be able to observe the finer and more subtle points of communication, including eye movements, facial expressions, postural shifts and hand gestures. Students sitting in the far upper reaches of large lecture theatres are likely to be too far away to pick up these cues. So, if you want to maximise your marks, sit in the front and listen. Leave the lovers, larrikins and the lost to their own pursuits.

It might be helpful to mention one other warm-up activity which will enhance your thinking and listening. If you have already scanned the text chapter and you still are waiting for the class to start, then page through the notes of your last lecture in that subject. Lectures are generally presented in a series, so that the end of the preceding class will most likely be the starting point for the next lecture. Having browsed through these notes, your mind will be warmed-up and ready to start when the lecture commences.

In summary, a small amount of time spent browsing through the relevant sections of your texts and perusing your previous lecture notes prior to each of your day's classes will reward you in several ways: your mind will be prepared; your listening will be more acute; and your notes will be more accurate and meaningful. The time investment is small; the dividends are great. As mentioned in a popular film, *The Godfather*, warming-up for your lectures is a deal which you can't refuse.

Practical pointers

- Be certain to obtain a syllabus for each subject you are

studying.

- Check the syllabus each week and note the topics to be covered for each class.
- Prior to your classes, browse through the relevant chapter of your text to familiarise yourself with the topics, ideas, key terms, charts and graphs.
- Just before the commencement of each lecture, scan your lecture notes from the preceding class.
- Sit where you can concentrate on the lecture and not be distracted. Front seats are generally better for distraction-free listening.
- Have at least two pens, one of which should be red, for taking notes. A highlighter might also be helpful.
- Concentrate on getting the major ideas from each lecture.
- If boredom becomes a problem, challenge your mind and anticipate in what direction the lecturer is proceeding. Ask yourself how the topic being presented might have personal application to you.
- Relax your mind while the lecturer is telling jokes or anecdotes, but don't relax too much. The rest period will be short and you will have to resume active listening.
- Your thinking speed will be about four to five times the lecturer's speaking speed (120–180 words per minute). It has been found that we spend about 27 minutes per wakeful hour listening, but only seven(!) minutes are spent in *effective* listening. Challenge yourself to listen effectively for most or all of your listening time.
- Listen for good examination questions. Lecturers have to ultimately set examinations and the questions are most likely to come from their lectures. Ask yourself what are the three most examinable topics being presented in this lecture. That should spur your mind into very discerning listening.

Practical exercises

If your listening skills are rusty, try the following exercises.

1 Think of the television news broadcasts as mini-lectures in contemporary history. In a popular media sense, that's exactly what they are. If you want to watch one or two news broadcasts each day, see them as lectures and take notes of the items being presented. You will have to work quickly, as the programming of these broadcasts is quick and fast moving. Your writing hand and your mind will be working very hard to keep up, but the practice will make you a much more agile and productive listener and note-taker in your lectures.

2 An exercise which you can do to increase your listening and concentration powers is to make a tape-recording of serial instructions. For example, imagine you are being given instructions as a traveller on how to find a particular place in an unfamiliar city. Ask a friend to make a tape with several sets of instructions, starting with a three-step series and progressing up to perhaps ten or more steps, a very difficult level of recall for most people. Having listened to the taped series, you then try to repeat the instructions. Here is an example: in order to get to the Post Office, go down High St for two blocks and turn right at the BP petrol station onto Bligh St. Go along Bligh St for three blocks and turn left at the City Library. The Post Office is midway along the block on Saddler St.

   Even though this is a brief set of instructions, it can be difficult listening to and concentrating upon the various steps so that you can remember the full set. A few hints at this stage might be helpful. Try to use as much visualisation as possible. Memory studies have shown that the more you can visualise, the better your memory. In the above example, see yourself proceeding along the various streets and picture in prominence the mentioned landmarks: the BP station, the City Library and finally the Post Office. Link the names of the streets to the images of the landmarks. With practice, you will be surprised at how well you can improve your listening powers and your immediate recall. These skills will certainly benefit you in your lectures.

3 Your concentration powers can even be strengthened as you fall off to sleep! For many people, getting to sleep is a chore because they allow their mind to wander off onto all of the worries and problems which have affected them that day—

or might affect them tomorrow. Try the following exercise to keep your mind concentrated and focused upon a sleep-inducing series of steps.

When you get into bed and want to drop off to sleep, focus your mind solely upon your breathing. Allow your breathing to become comfortably slow and steady. When ready, say to yourself, '100' as you breathe in. Visualise the number being drawn in your mind as you say it to yourself. As you breathe out, say 'relax'. Next breath in, say '99' and 'relax' as you breathe out. Try to concentrate on the series and count steadily down to say 75. You will find yourself drifting off. However, keep your mind riveted to the number series and don't let any competing thoughts intrude. You will find your mental control capabilities increasing over the next weeks and months. You will also get to sleep much more quickly.

4
Note-taking

- Warming up before your lectures
- Becoming a more efficient note-taker
- The structure of lectures
- Revising soon after the lectures
- Learning your lecture notes week by week
- Revising your notes before your exams
- Glossary of note-taking symbols and abbreviations

Lectures have been the traditional form of communicating information in higher education institutions for hundreds of years. While an argument could be made for other forms of teaching, the lecture seems to be a firmly entrenched educational practice.

Josie was an enthusiastic first-year university student who was living in one of the campus colleges. She became involved in a whirlwind social life within the first weeks on campus and found that the late night bull sessions interfered with her lecture attendance anytime before 11.00 am. When she did arrive for these 'early' lectures, she was often late and poorly equipped (no pen, the wrong note pad, and certainly no previous warm-up for the lecture topics). After finding a pen from a willing neighbour, Josie took notes on wrinkled bits of notepaper, in between exchanging gossip and making arrangements for her next weekend party activities. When the mid-semester exams arrived, Josie was still having a ball, but she was very poorly equipped academically. The odd bits of notes which she could locate resembled hieroglyphics (and she wasn't studying Egyptology). During the exams, she realised she had absolutely no chance of passing. Fortunately, she responded to this early crisis and sought counselling.

Josie's plight is not unusual. Many students do not know how to make the best use of the lecture situation. Your major job as a student is to listen *actively* during the presentation and to take down a good set of lecture notes. If you are uncertain of the difference between active listening and just hearing, see the preceding chapter. Active listening is the basis for effective note-taking.

You might well ask why take notes during the lectures. Mainly because your brain will undergo a perfectly normal leakage in short-term memory of about 80 per cent in 24 hours. That means you will hold in your short-term memory only about 20 per cent of the content of any lecture one day later. That leakage will continue as time progresses, meaning that your recall could well be next to nothing by exam time. Walking into an exam with little if any recall of the lectures is an agonising form of academic suicide.

The solution to the memory leakage problem is prevention. It's just like preventing a leaking tap from draining a crucial water tank. You simply put a washer in the system to keep the water supply safe. Instead of putting washers into your brain, I am suggesting putting revision into your notes. That will help to halt the leakage. To obtain the best possible set of lecture notes, you should start well before your lectures commence. Let's look at the important steps in the note-taking process.

Obtain a syllabus for every subject being studied

Most courses these days will have a syllabus which outlines the scope of the topics to be covered during the lecture series. The syllabus might also include the weeks when the topics will be covered and recommended readings in key references. A final and very important feature of the course syllabus is a guide to how you will be assessed. All of these features make the course syllabus a very important student resource to be used throughout the academic semester. If, perchance, your lecturer does not distribute a syllabus, it is perfectly reasonable to tactfully ask if one is to be provided.

Warm up your mind before each lecture

Most athletes who train regularly would strongly advise any contender at the championships to warm up thoroughly prior to competing. Why? Because the muscles of your body work much more efficiently when they are warm and the ample blood supply is providing a ready source of oxygen. The warming-up process also helps to prevent sprains and other sport injuries.

The same principle applies to warming up the brain prior to your lectures. However, the rationale for warming-up is more cognitive than physiological. Your mind is not going to generate an oxygen deficit during most ordinary lectures and the brain cells are not likely to incur any injuries. However, your mind will certainly benefit from some preparatory exercise prior to your lectures.

Most students unfortunately walk into their lectures without any familiarisation of the topics to be covered. It's much like standing on the steps at a city railway station trying to meet a person you do not know. Thousands of people flow from the doorway and you survey the faces. As you are not familiar with the person to be met, one face seems much like the next. Your task proves to be more difficult and more perplexing than need be. The solution: know what to look for. In the example at the railway station, a photograph would be very handy.

For the students who have not prepared prior to the lecture, all of the ideas, terms and concepts being presented might well blend into the other words and seem to be a vegetable soup. However, the prepared student has the distinct advantage of recognising the important terms and concepts when they are introduced during the lecture. While the unprepared students are either frantic or confused, the students who have warmed up are calmly getting on with their note-taking in an effective and efficient manner.

The warming-up process is really just a short browse through the reference source. As mentioned earlier, the reference is very likely to be included in the syllabus. Find the chapter or section pertaining to the topics scheduled for the next lecture and run your eyes down each page. Note any topic which is in **bold-face** print, *italics*, or is included as a section heading or title to a chart or graph. These are topics which the editors have probably designed to 'jump off the page' and thus make the material more readable. You might want to question in your mind what does this term mean and how does it relate to the other terms being presented in this chapter. You might also want to write the term in a notebook just to graphically lodge it in your mind. The whole warming-up process should take only about five to ten minutes.

Having browsed the reference material, your task in the lecture will be made much easier as you will know what is important. Most students who have not done any pre-lecture browsing will be caught in a state of frequent stress trying to decide whether to take notes on a particular topic or to leave it. Having familiarised yourself with the material, you can proceed confidently with your note-taking and avoid this state of indecisiveness.

In addition to browsing through the reference chapter, another warming-up process which is particularly helpful is reviewing the notes of your preceding lecture. As lectures are generally presented in series, the present lecture will probably pickup where the previous one finished. In the few minutes before the start of each lecture, run your eyes over your previous lecture notes to refresh your mind about the topics which were covered. You are then ready to start in an informed state when the lecturer begins.

Thus, warming up your mind has many advantages: it starts the learning process early; it equips you to be more selective and decisive in your note-taking; and it helps you to produce a better set of notes.

Efficient note-taking

Jennifer was a 42-year-old mature age student who had previously worked for many years as a shorthand stenographer and private secretary in a multinational legal firm. She prided herself on being very thorough and she looked forward to using her very proficient shorthand skills during her lectures. Jennifer attended every lecture and took down in her notebook every umm, ahh, joke, anecdote and quip uttered by each lecturer. At the end of each day, she transcribed the lectures and produced by the end of the semester four impressive volumes, one for each of the subjects she was studying.

While these transcriptions were very neatly presented and totally comprehensive, Jennifer had one major problem—she worked so long and so hard at producing them that she did not have adequate time to learn the notes. The problem was compounded by the fact that there were simply too many notes. Perhaps 20 per cent of what was recorded and later transcribed was irrelevant.

The solution was fairly straightforward. Having learned that she had to become more selective and discriminating in her note-taking, Jennifer made a firm practice of preparing prior to each lecture so that she could recognise the essential terms and concepts when they were presented. Her shorthand skills were still used, but selectively so. With a prepared mind and practised hand, she was able to obtain an excellent set of notes. She continued to transcribe the shorthand notes, even though this process is *not* recommended. For most students, writing notes again is too time consuming. However, her typing speed minimised the time expenditure and she claimed that the transcription process was a learning experience, which in fact it probably was.

The lesson to be learned from Jennifer's case is that recording too many notes can be almost as problematic as not having enough. The key strategies are to prepare your mind before the lecture and then be selective in what you take down in your notes. For best results, it might be helpful to look at the overall structure of most lectures so that you can recognise the critical parts.

The structure of most lectures

While every lecture will vary somewhat in the style and format, most lectures can be conveniently divided into three basic parts: the introduction, the body and the summary. Let's look at each in turn.

The introduction is presented at the very start of the lecture and generally comprises a brief overview of what will be discussed in the body. When there is a series of lectures being presented on a given subject, some lecturers might present a brief summary of what has been presented in the preceding lecture(s) to help you get oriented. Whatever the actual content, the introduction is a prime opportunity for you to warm up for the presentation. Your mind should be listening acutely for any mention of the terms and concepts which were (one hopes) noted when you browsed through the reference sources prior to the lecture. As mentioned earlier, the very fact that you recognise several of these key terms will cause them to have a much greater impact upon your mind.

In addition to getting your mind into gear for the lecture, the introduction is also the time for you to be organising the essential equipment which will be necessary to get a good set of notes. The fundamentals hardly need mentioning, but for completeness, let me say that you will certainly need at least two pens (Murphy's Law states that your pen will run dry just at the most critical point in the lecture). One of the pens might be red. You might also want to bring a highlighter. You then have the means to emphasise certain terms for later attention.

Try various types of note-taking 'systems', including loose-leaf tablets on clipboard, bound notebooks, or different types of filing folders. Having tried most of the range, I found the loose-leaf paper and clipboard to be the most flexible. While speaking of paper, you might need some graph/log paper, lined paper or coloured paper, depending upon the subjects you are studying. If you choose the loose-leaf method, select paper with reinforced holes for secure filing in your notebooks. Your campus or local stationery store will be able to supply most of your needs.

Other types of equipment which might be necessary include ruler, compass, and calculator, once again depending upon the nature of your studies. Arriving at a lecture and not having the requisite equipment will cause some anxiety and considerable inconvenience. You will not boost your popularity rating amongst your classmates if you insist on borrowing their equipment during lectures on more than one occasion.

Having discussed what happens during the introduction and how to get set for active note-taking, let's look at the body of the lecture, the section in most lectures where the key concepts are presented.

The body of most lectures will vary, depending upon the discipline. For example, science and mathematics lectures will often be quite straightforward. There might be problems presented with various steps for arriving at solutions. Or, there might be lists of characteristics or charts and graphs describing some phenomenon. Generally, there is no doubt about the major concept being discussed and there will often be a clear approach to the presentation.

While science-based lectures might tend to be clear, some lectures in the arts and humanities might be more discursive. That is, you might experience some difficulty differentiating what are the crucial points from the more illustrative or tangential aspects. That is not to say that lecturers in these disciplines are less clear thinking. It is just the nature of the topics being presented.

The task for students in all types of lectures is to get a good set of notes. Basically, you will have to tune your mind to think analytically and selectively to obtain the best results. Keep your mind on target by asking both analytical and selective questions. What is the meaning of this term? How does this concept relate to the one just presented? What causes this phenomenon to occur? What are the future implications or ramifications of this event? These questions help you to extend your thinking and obtain a better understanding of the lecture. They will also keep you awake!

The final part of most lectures is a summary of what was just presented. Many students respond to the words, 'In summary . . .' as a signal to turn off mentally, slap their notebook shut and head for the exit. Those who stay put and look over their notes as the lecturer recapitulates will find that they derive considerable benefit from this brief investment of time and attention. It is the prime opportunity to locate any areas of omission or confusion. If you discover a point of poor understanding, then approach the lecturer straightaway and try to get it explained. If you do not have the opportunity immediately, then see the lecturer as soon as possible later that day.

Concentrating during lectures

Where do you think the students who gain the highest marks sit in a lecture theatre or classroom? Those who have read Chapter 3 already know. Most other readers with any tertiary experience will say right in the front rows. They are absolutely correct.

Let's say that you are sitting in an optimal position for listening actively to the lecturer, but the basic problem is boredom. Even the most scintillating lecturers can seem boring at times. One of the problems is that most people speak at between 120 and 180 words per minute, but your mind can process words at about four times as fast. If you find boredom setting in, try to prompt more attention by guessing where the lecture is going. Challenge your mind by asking what relationships exist between the present topic and the preceding ones. Ask yourself about the ramifications of lecture topics presented so far. If you have an egocentric bias (and we all do to some extent), ask yourself how the topic being discussed relates directly to you. Any question you ask yourself is likely to improve your concentration. If all else fails, the time-honoured self-administered pinch can do wonders. The following case study is typical.

Ben was a third-year technical college student studying for a diploma in mechanical engineering. He consulted me because he had failed several subjects twice and was being asked by his department to justify his readmission. During the interview, Ben said that even though he was very committed to mechanical engineering, he questioned within himself whether he had the ability to do well in the field. As his confidence began to wane, so did his concentration.

The approach taken with Ben is probably applicable to most students whose lecture room concentration is weak. You will hear about the Rule of 3 several times in this book, and this is your first instalment. I suggested to Ben that he attend every lecture and no matter what his mood might be, he ask himself several times what are the three most examinable points being presented in this lecture. That question had both immediate and longer term relevance to him. It spurred his concentration there and then and helped him to identify topics which could win him marks at the next examination.

In addition to the Rule of 3, I strongly recommended that he prepare for every lecture and that he liaise with his teaching staff about any difficulties he might be having. Previously, he avoided the staff because he thought they would think he was dumb if he asked for a concept to be explained again. He was surprised to find that the staff were both friendly and eager to help. The outcome of Ben's dilemma was that he was re-admitted to his course and eventually graduated. At a follow-up interview after he had started work, he mentioned that he still applies the Rule of 3 when receiving complicated instructions or sitting in long meetings. Learning how to listen and concentrate in his college lectures was of considerable help in the longer term.

Handling overheads

Most students will be very familiar with the overhead projector which is now a standard piece of teaching equipment found in virtually every lecture hall and classroom. While the overhead projector has allowed teaching staff to prepare neat and clear notes prior to their classes, this teaching aid has presented some problems for students. The basic difficulty is that the lecturer can proceed at what might seem to be a blistering pace, slapping a rapid series of transparencies onto the projector to a chorus of moans and groans from the students who cannot keep pace.

There are several ways you can cope more effectively with this familiar problem. Firstly, be prepared for these lectures.

Know your texts and reference sources. If you recognise a graph or chart and do not have time to get all of the details, get the title of the graph and note in the margin, *See text for graph.* That evening you can transfer the chart into your notes at a more comfortable pace. There is a second strategy to consider. Lecturers will often present essentially the same lectures year after year with small updating changes. Ask former students who performed well in the subject if you might use their lecture notes as a briefing medium to help you cope better. Thirdly, if you still find it difficult to keep pace, discuss the problem with other classmates and consider seeing the lecturer as a group and suggest a slightly slower lecture pace.

Note-taking speed

Not everyone will have the opportunity to learn formal short-hand, but you can develop your own system. Basically, you will want to devise a range of symbols and abbreviations which allow you to take notes more efficiently. You will most likely be familiar with the mathematical symbols for addition, subtraction, multiplication and division. Science students will be familiar with the use of horizontal arrows indicating yields and vertical arrows symbolising gases. What is being suggested is that you develop your own set of symbols which relate to the common terms, concepts and procedures frequently encountered in your lectures. A sample glossary of notetaking symbols and their meanings is set out below. Start your own glossary and as new and frequently used terms emerge in your lectures, devise a symbol or abbreviation and record it in your glossary so that you know the meaning when your notes are being revised.

$\rightarrow$ leads to, causes, direction
$\uparrow$ increase, much, elevate, high
$\downarrow$ decrease, descend, low, little, few
$\leftrightarrow$ both ways, either way
$=$ equal ϕ birth
$\approx$ approximately $\dagger$ death
$\therefore$ therefore $\Rightarrow$ implies
$\male$ male, $\male$ father $\because$ because
$\female$ female, $\female$ mother   b/w between

> greater than	× times, multiply
< less than	@ at, each
≠ unequal	& and
Δ change	c̄ with
+ add to, plus	re about
− take away, subtract	WRT with respect to
÷ divide	

Subject-specific abbreviations
EEG electroencephalograph
GNP gross national product

Silence, a signal?

Good lecturers will often use long pauses and silence for various purposes: to give emphasis to a particular point just presented; and to allow students some time to get an important or complicated point down into their notes. Unfortunately, some students act more like robots who respond only to verbal stimuli. That is, when the talking stops, they stop. In order to get the best possible set of notes, be alert to the possible implications of pauses and silences. They are often there for your benefit.

There are also certain key words which should cause caution lights to flash in your mind. They include: *examinable, assessable, must know,* and any other term which suggests that the present concept is very important and it's likely to appear on an examination paper.

Practical pointers to obtain good lecture notes

- Know what topics will be presented. Consult your syllabus and browse through the reference materials before each lecture.
- Note the title of the lecture, the lecturer's name, and the date on the first page of your notes.
- Number your pages in case they get out of order or dislodged from your notebook.
- Leave plenty of open space on each page for supplementary notes.
- Organise your notes as you listen. If you prefer an outlining

approach, then number and letter as you go.

- Have several different coloured pens available plus a highlighter to make important points more prominent.
- Make notes to yourself in the margins, such as, *Know for exams! Good essay question topic. Unclear. Get help.*
- Be sure to note special diagrams, charts and graphs. If there is not sufficient time to record them entirely, ask the lecturer for the reference.
- Be flexible and adapt to the lecturer's presentation style.
- Avoid rewriting your notes. It's very time consuming. Improve your note-taking skills to obtain the best possible notes during each lecture.
- Should ancillary notes be needed, write the supplementary information on small slips of paper and tape them to the top, bottom and free side of your note sheets to obtain a complete treatment on the topics.
- When the lectures are dealing with complex issues and intricate diagrams or charts, consider taking your text or reference source to class with you.

For maximum marks ...

Do you recall what percentage of information leaks from your short-term memory in 24 hours? Rather than go scrambling through the earlier pages, it's 80 per cent. That means by the weekend, your recall of most of the lecture content of the preceding week will be scraping bottom. In order to get your memory cells working for you, you will have to be willing to tolerate a bit of hard work. In order to obtain high marks on your exams, reserve a few hours *each weekend* and go through your lecture notes and *learn* them as if you were going to be examined the following Monday. Learning as you go requires discipline, but the results are beyond dispute. Periodic learning is far superior to cramming, even though cramming has been a student tradition for hundreds of years.

Exam day will arrive, no matter what you do. That's when the bulk of marks are either going to be won or lost. Your notes will be your major study resource, but you will need to work your way through them at least four to five times. Most students manage once or twice, but that will only get them to the level of familiarity. If you want to do well, you will want to be more than just casually familiar with your notes—ideally, you will want to know them thoroughly.

Think of your knowledge level as a handful of dry sand. If you walk into the exam room and begin to get nervous and shake just a bit, the sand will fall from between your fingers. Metaphorically speaking, it's much better to enter the exams with your knowledge symbolised as rock-hard granite. No matter how much shivering and shaking you might experience, the granite will not crumble—there will be no breakdown in your recall. Remember, that rock-hard knowledge comes with many revisions of your notes and that will take considerable time, perhaps several weeks. Get started on those revisions four to six weeks before the end of the academic term.

Thus, lectures will be a critical source of learning and your lecture notes will be the major medium for exam preparation. Be certain to warm up for each lecture by familiarising yourself with the concepts to be presented. Sit in the front rows to maximise hearing and viewing (and marks). Be well equipped to cope with the different types of note-taking. Revise the notes from previous lectures while waiting for the lecture to begin. Keep your mind alert by asking analytical questions. Revise your notes as soon as possible after the lecture and be prepared to go over them at least four to five times before your exams.

Practical exercises

1 Start a personal glossary of note-taking symbols and abbreviations. Put them into practice by using them as often as possible.
2 Exchange note-taking ideas with your classmates. Find out what symbols and abbreviations they use to help speed up their note-taking. Jot down their symbols so you can add them to your personal glossary.
3 As suggested in the previous chapter, practise taking notes during TV news broadcasts. The practice will increase your note-taking skill and speed.
4 Always strive to take notes in your academic meetings, including lectures, tutorials, seminars, laboratory sessions and even informal discussions with staff and other students.

5 If you want to take your note-taking to higher levels of achievement, enroll in a shorthand course, but realise your aim is to be selective in what you note. You do not want a record of every utterance of the lecturer.

5
Reading more efficiently

- Speed reading—the harsh realities
- Scanning
- Reading to learn and retain
- Revision reading for exams
- Practical exercises

We are faced with an information avalanche. Present-day students often find that they have say, fifteen hours of reading to do but only six hours of available time. The following week, there is another nine hours of carried over reading to add to the next lot of fifteen. For many, that ever-increasing backlog of reading is a formula for academic stress. A very common scenario is manifest in the case of Rob who initially saw me about speed reading.

Rob was enrolled in a civil engineering diploma at Technical College. He had 26 class contact hours per week and on top of that he worked fifteen hours each weekend for a cleaning firm. Time for reading and studying were very limited. Four weeks into his first year of study, he had a reading list two pages long. It looked absolutely insurmountable. Every lecturer in his nine different subjects had given lengthy lists of recommended readings accompanying the syllabus. In his conscientious fashion, he tried to do the reading, but he was just getting further and further behind.

Part of Rob's problem was that he tried to read everything on the lists and with the same word by word method. There were two basic issues which we discussed: one, his reading method was very slow, and two, he used only one reading technique for all reading matter. During our sessions, we discussed a variety of reading techniques which then allowed him to be more adaptable and efficient. A practical prompter which he obtained from our first session was a self-directed question: How should I read this? The 'how' implied different reading techniques which could be used with different types of reading matter. Reciting that question prompted Rob to become a more selective and efficient reader. Before going into various types of reading approaches, let's look firstly at the theory of speed reading.

The theory of speed reading

Just as with Rob, many students see speed reading as the easy answer to the ever growing pile of texts, references and resource papers which 'must be read'. Let's clear up some popular misconceptions right from the start. Speed reading is not the definitive answer to most academic survival problems. And, even if it were, it certainly is not an easy skill to obtain or practise. Inspite of these qualifications, you may still want to know how to speed read. Here's how it works.

Basically, speed reading is a function of the number of eye fixations, or momentary stops, which you experience as you move your eyes across a line of writing. Even though one fixation is a very brief pause in your eye movements, usually a matter of micro-seconds, the cumulative total of these fixations can be immense. Most inexperienced readers will have up to eight to ten eye fixations per average line of text. When you multiply the fixation times for each line by the total number of lines to be read, the figure can be justifiably concerning. Basically, for most students with an average reading load, you are looking at many hours per week of extra reading time—and that's time during which the eyes are at a dead stop.

If eye fixations are one of the basic problems (I'll address some others below), what can be done about them? The answer is to reduce them. That is, train your eyes to take in more of the line at each fixation. Think of your eyes as being the end of a vacuum cleaner hose. Metaphorically speaking, most students poke the nozzle down on the line of writing eight to ten times and suck up the letters in the immediate vicinity. Extending the metaphor, the more efficient readers use a wide applicator and are able to draw in many more words and use far fewer pokes or fixations. The true masters of speed reading are reputed to *run* their eyes down the middle of the page and suck up the essential words on both sides. While this is theoretically possible, it is extraordinarily difficult. For some types of reading matter, such as technical, mathematical or logically complex material, it may not be applicable at all.

So, with most general types of reading matter, the secret is to pause less frequently and to widen your visual field. Sounds straightforward, but how do you do it? Practice. Some indication of what practice can do might be gleaned from this personal experience. I attended a university preparation program prior to starting my first degree and we spent two one-hour sessions per day practising reading acceleration. I entered the three-week program with a reading speed of 350 words per minute and in three weeks increased it to 1000. That was a very pleasing result, but only achieved with some pain and suffering. The twice daily practice sessions required very rigorous concentration, almost to the point of having sweat dripping from my brow, but the hard work was worth it.

There are some limitations which should be mentioned. You will not really be able to speed read everything. As suggested above, running your eyes at a blistering pace down a page of equations is unlikely to produce a clear understanding of the mathematical concept. Any detailed subject which requires logical and progressive understanding from step to step is not going to be a speed reading project. Thinking and understanding take time, so plan your reading method with both the reading material and your desired end result in mind.

Betty was a third-year physics major who was wanting to improve her study skills and overall efficiency. She approached a commercial speed reading firm and they assured her that she would be able to increase her reading speed by at least 200 per cent. The cost of the course was prohibitive, so she enquired about other sources of help.

Betty was a very talented student. She had been achieving distinctions in her academic work and wanted to strive for high distinctions. She profited from one particular suggestion—that she scan each reading task before actually commencing detailed reading. Sounds simple, and I must say that scanning is reasonably straightforward—and for a change, not difficult.

Scanning

Basically, the process of scanning involves running your eyes down each page and taking note of any terms in **bold-face** print or *italics*, section headings, graphs and charts or anything else which seems to jump off the page. Most textbooks and student resources are designed to be very reader-friendly. That is, the author and editors make every effort to help the student learn from the resource. Some texts even have margin notes to tell you what the section is about.

While you are scanning the chapter or section, your mind will have to be very alert and active. Your eyes act only as the collectors of information—your mind must do the registering and analysing. As you scan down the page, ask yourself the following questions. What does this term mean? What relationship does it have to the preceding concepts? What is its importance? These types of questions help to give that specific term some discrete relevance and significance. However, if you can not provide immediate answers to the above questions, do not get bogged down. Scanning is a preliminary process, an initial exposure without expectation of thorough understanding. You just want to get the basic drift of the reading material and mentally note some of the important terms.

If it helps, you might want to make a note of the terms picked up by scanning. Remember, writing is a time-consuming task. Write the term, not a definition. Just the act of writing the term will help to record it in your memory.

Why should you scan your reading material? You may recall from the lecture note-taking chapter that browsing through the background references prior to a lecture will help you listen and understand. The same processes are working in the scanning process. Having noted several terms and concepts during the scanning process, your mind will be primed for their presence during the reading function. When you come upon these important terms, they have a much greater impact than if you were to read the material cold.

Scanning techniques

During my third undergraduate year, I had the task of reading twenty books followed by an oral exam on each. I recall having run out of time on *The Microbe Hunters* and finding that I was obliged to attend the oral exam on the book the following day. That meant reading the book in one night, a challenge to any speed reader. I decided to read the introductory section and the final few paragraphs of each chapter hoping that any crucial information would be found in those sections. Surprisingly, I passed the oral exam.

Perhaps the basis for this particular scanning approach is that any well-written text often tells you the message at least three times. The introduction gives you the overview, the body provides the detailed treatment, and the finishing paragraphs generally provide a summary. Having scanned the first and last sections of each chapter, I at least was able to get two out of the three messages. It seemed to work, but I do not recommend reading a work for the first time the night before an exam.

Another scanning technique which might be helpful is to read the first sentence of each paragraph. Once again, well-written works often have lead sentences introducing the concept being dealt with in the paragraph. This will not always be the case, but for scanning purposes, you will probably obtain the general drift of the work.

A final approach which you might have an opportunity to use is what I call the magnetic technique. Think of your eyes as magnets and run them down the page. Allow them to be drawn to **bold-face** print, *italics*, or any other terms which stand out from the surrounding text. As you can see, this is a much more cursory approach, but with practice, you will be able to glean the essence from the text in very short order.

In summary, scanning is a very efficient and most helpful set of reading techniques which allow you to get the overview of the material or to find specific facts quite quickly. You will want to use different approaches for different types of writing and for different types of reading goals. The point to be stressed is that scanning will save you time.

Reading to learn and retain information

Margaret was a first-year university Arts student who claimed she could not retain the information she was reading for her course. She said she could read a chapter of political science or sociology and have very little knowledge of the material at the end. Not only was this very frustrating for her, but it also eroded her confidence.

We discussed her reading technique which was a word by word vocalising approach (she pronounced each word to herself as she progressed). Margaret said she always had read that way.

The technique which I suggested to Margaret is called the SQ3R approach. That is an acronym standing for *survey, question, read, recite, review.* Let's look at each of the individual processes in turn.

The *survey* function is just like the warm-up preview which was described in the chapter on warming up to listen effectively in your lectures. Instead of preparing your mind to listen, you are now obtaining an overview for increased understanding and recall of reading material. The actual process is much the same. Take perhaps five minutes to simply browse through the pages noting the important terms. The **bold-face** print and any *italics* should take your attention. Also ponder the graphs, charts and any other visual aids.

The *question* process of the SQ3R technique suggests that

during the survey phase you turn the terms which you note into questions. Suppose you are surveying a chapter on photosynthesis in biology and you come across the terms chlorophyll and light and dark reactions. While mentally noting these terms, construct questions about them. What is chlorophyll? How does it relate to photosynthesis? These questions will serve to give special prominence to the important terms you note during the survey process.

The next process is *read*. Because you are reading to retain, you will want to understand the material. Some reading matter will be straightforward and some will be extremely difficult. I recall trying to read the works of two philosophers, Locke and Hume, and finding the work very difficult going indeed. After the first reading I was mystified. Following the second, I was still confused. During the third (and final) attempt, I began to question my basic ability. I was saved from this mental torment by two classmates who also found the readings difficult, but whose views, when added to mine, made the readings more clear. Just in passing, when you're frustrated by a difficulty like this, talk it over with several close classmates. You will probably find an equal amount of confusion which helps to dispel any thoughts that you're dumb.

Now, back to the reading process. When you set yourself a reading task, break it up into small bits. Reading a full chapter at one go is much more difficult than reading a series of, say, seven small sections. The benefit of reading section by section is that you pause after each section and consolidate your thoughts.

The consolidation process brings us to the next reading step, *recite*. Having just finished reading the first section of a chapter or assignment, pause and recite the major ideas. You might use the Rule of 3 here. Ask yourself what are the three most important points covered in the section. If you can not name any points, your mind has probably been daydreaming and you had better re-read the section.

The recitation process helps to fix the concept more firmly in your memory. As you proceed through the subsequent sections, pause and recite the central points to yourself. If noting the terms on paper helps to make a greater impression, then do so, but remember to limit your writing to just the key terms. As mentioned previously, writing takes valuable time.

The final step in reading for retention is *review*. It might sound dreary having to go back over the material, but that is exactly how you will increase your learning. That familiar expression, 'Repetition is a great teacher', is founded upon this process. Go back and logically link the central ideas from each of the reading sections. This process will not only help you remember the individual points, it will also give you a more sound and thorough understanding of the overall concept.

Revising the material you have just read should take only several minutes. That small amount of time will be very well spent as your understanding will be expanded and your memory will be reinforced.

Revision reading for exams

With reference to your final results, probably the most important type of reading will be revision reading for your examinations. As suggested in the note-taking chapter, the ideal time to begin the revising and learning of your lecture notes is immediately after each lecture. At this time, you will have optimal chances of recalling any missed facts or ideas. You are also able to reinforce any points of emphasis presented by the lecturer.

To maximise your learning, try to read and learn your lecture notes each weekend. That sounds draconian, but the research evidence on systematic, spaced learning is beyond dispute. Regrettably, most students overlook this opportunity and cram all of their learning into the final week or two prior to their exams. Time is limited during these panic-stricken weeks and as a result, many students enter their examinations knowing that they are inadequately prepared.

Looking on the brighter side, let's assume that you have been reading through your notes each weekend. By examination time, most of the central ideas and concepts will have been firmly embedded in your mind. It is important to state that firm learning will have occurred because of the opportunity to reinforce and *use* the information. Remember—*information used is information retained.*

The essential goal during the pre-exam period is to revise your notes and other materials at least three or more times. If you have been learning as you go, then a good three revisions will allow you to polish your understanding of the concepts. If, however, you have let the revision slide until the pre-exam period, you will need to find time to read and revise your notes perhaps five or more times.

Strategically, the best way to approach your revision is to quickly survey all materials. Look for items of prime importance—the highly examinable topics—and give them special attention. A second strategy is to specifically adapt your revision to the individual subjects being studied. For example, arts and humanities subjects are generally best revised by reading over and over the notes many times. Expect the first and second readings to be a bit of a blur, but the subsequent readings should make the concepts more understandable and memorable. You will want to know important definitions and the relationships existing being central ideas and concepts. Test yourself as you progress. One very helpful pointer is to think of yourself as the examiner and list the three most examinable points of each lecture. That will sharpen your perception and should also enhance your motivation.

Mathematics and science subjects will require a different approach. Following a quick survey of your notes, lab reports and other materials, read through the theory topics and learn them thoroughly. You will want to go over the concepts so that you not only know the topics A, B, and C very well, but also the relationships A–B, B–C, and A–C. Good examiners are likely to examine the latter relationships more than the individual topics.

In addition to the theory, you will also have to address the sample problems which were included in the lectures, tutorials or laboratory sessions. Most exams in mathematics and science will have a problem-solving section and there is only one way to prepare—solve lots of practice problems, preferably correctly. Problem solving is a much more time-consuming task and for that reason, it is important to start your revision early. Indeed, the problem solving should be carried out weekly so that the knowledge gained in week one is able to be used in week two, and so on. If you strike a snag anywhere along the line, be certain to get help and sort the matter out quickly. A point of difficulty experienced in week three, for example, can produce an absolute avalanche of confusion by week six.

Where do you find the time to do all of this examination revision? You might have to make the time, that is deleting something else from your schedule and inserting several revision sessions. Remember, the most important factor in examination success is thorough revision. Therefore, if you are serious about succeeding in your studies, then be certain to make the time for examination preparation. A systematic approach of revising each weekend over one term of study will prove how beneficial this strategy is.

Summary

Speed reading is a function of taking in a wider span of words at each eye fixation point while reading across a line of text. You can generally improve your reading speed, but you will have to practise this visual field expansion procedure and be prepared to work very hard at concentration.

Scanning is a very helpful and timesaving reading technique. Scanning can provide an overview before you read in more detail. It is also useful when looking quickly through a chapter or book to find the specific material you are wanting to read about in detail. You look generally for the key words and concepts.

Reading to learn and retain is hard work and is best pursued using the SQ3R technique. *Survey* the section; formulate *questions* in your mind about the key concepts and terms; *read* the material section by section; pause after each section and *recite* the major points of that section; and *revise* as you go, linking the terms and concepts of one section to the next. The procedure takes time and perseverance, but it works!

Revision reading for exams should be started at the end of Week One and slotted in as a regular weekend study task. Go over your notes and other study materials many times, but a minimum of three or four times is likely to be required before you acquire a sound knowledge of the material.

Practical exercises

- Practise speed reading every time you read a newspaper or any other leisure reading material. Try to run your eyes as rapidly as possible down the columns and extract the key concepts and facts.

- Train your eyes to look for the critical nouns in any academic reading. Filter out the articles and prepositions, such as: the, an, a, on, in, at, etc. Rarely will these words be of any significant import to the concepts being read.
- Before any reading exercise, scan the entire article, chapter or section which you intend to read. Warm up your mind by mentally noting the key terms and concepts.

6
Library research skills

- Know the anatomy of your library
- Know how your library works
- Saving time in library research
- Practical exercises

Greg was a final-year high school student who was wanting to pursue a teaching career after completing a university Arts/Education degree. His final year at high school consisted of several major assessable essay tasks plus the Higher School Certificate examination. As the assessable tasks contributed heavily to his final HSC score, it was important to perform well on these assignments.

Greg lived near a large university and he wanted to use the library to extend the research he had done on his essay assignments. When he entered the university library, he was intimidated by the size and apparent complexity of the place. There were numerous service counters, masses of people, a multiplicity of computer terminals, direction signs, stairwells to unknown departments and hallways disappearing into the distance. Greg stood in the centre of this maze feeling very uncertain about where he should start.

Much like a traveller in a foreign country, Greg looked around for a source of help. He felt nervous and conspicuous, thinking he was the only person there who did not know what to do. His apprehension was dispelled after slowly approaching the counter marked 'Readers' Assistance Unit'. The person on duty said in a friendly way, 'You look a bit lost. Can I help?' Greg explained what he wanted to do and the librarian gave him a map and several departments and people to contact. Having some basic information in hand and avenues to pursue, he felt more settled and secure.

Finding the relevant library resources and extracting the necessary information was not exactly easy going, but at least Greg knew help was at hand. He was also consoled by the fact that many students found libraries and their systems to be geographic challenges (the librarian exercised some poetic licence, choosing the term, 'inspirational adventure'). Coming down from lofty poetic expressions to ground-floor reality, the first step towards understanding how the system works is trying it—having a go.

While this brief chapter can not do justice to the very sophisticated and quite complex systems which comprise a contemporary library, it will present several helpful topics for students organising their library research activities. The underlying theme of this chapter will be time management, a constant challenge for most students.

Time traps in your library research

Greg's time for library research was very limited. His time problems were compounded by his lack of knowledge about the complex library system.

Whether at secondary or tertiary level, most students will fall into various types of time traps when conducting their library research. The major traps which warrant discussion are: failure to understand the basic operating procedures of the library; uncertainty about the general layout of the library; and inability to operate the information search equipment.

As only an occasional user of the library, it was not possible for Greg to participate in the orientation tours held earlier that year. However, all students should certainly do this when they start their studies at a school, college or university. The small amount of time spent touring the facilities will pay copious dividends when you begin researching activities in the library.

In place of the orientation tour, Greg was given a leaflet describing the library's layout and various functions. With the map and department descriptions in hand, Greg was able to find his way to the relevant sections and ultimately to the specific stacks. He left the library with far more confidence than when he entered. I should add that most of the confidence came from asking relevant questions of the various staff members.

Ann, a classmate of Greg's, was less courageous. She was initially confused by the size and complexity of the library, but she chose to try to work it out on her own. She spent hours wandering here and there and left with only a few articles relating to her assignment.

Why was Ann's visit so unproductive? Primarily because she advanced her social life at the expense of her project research. Ann found several people she had known previously and her research time became compromised, a very common trap for many students. Perhaps it was the frustration of not immediately finding the books and articles she wanted; or then, maybe it was just her appealing and outgoing personality. Whatever the reason, her wanderings seemed to generate more social conversation than academic inspiration. At the end of her non-productive afternoon, she left the library unfulfilled, but with the offer of a movie date for the following weekend. At least the afternoon was a social success.

From a librarian's viewpoint, the essential difference between the two experiences of Greg and Ann was the willingness to ask questions of the staff. Greg's openness to say to the library staff, 'I'm lost' brought helpful directions and answers to his research questions. Ann's reticence simply generated frustration and further confusion. The moral of these two experiences: when in doubt or when confused, ask a library staff member.

One final time trap worthy of mention is queuing. At pre-exam time when the library's resources are usually at peak demand, many students will stand for long periods in queues waiting for various services, especially photocopying. There are two principles to mention here. Firstly, queuing is best avoided—try to get to the library at off-peak times. If you must stand in a queue, do so productively—read while standing. The second principle relates to photocopying directly. Resist the temptation to photocopy all articles which you think are relevant, if only tangentially so. You can save yourself money by skimming through the articles when you locate them. Try to summarise them straightaway rather than photocopy them for reading at some other time. The photocopy machine suppliers will not agree, but too much money is spent by students photocopying articles, many of which are never read. Save both time and money by reading the material quickly. Take your notes and move onto the next article. Don't take pictures of papers which might not be relevant.

Getting to know your library's layout

One of the most important orientation activities for incoming students is the library tour. Most campuses conduct an orientation program for new students and the library is generally a featured focus of activity. Trained staff take new students through the library and explain the functions of the various departments. The tour will probably include information about: finding books, articles and other reference materials; how to borrow materials; the use of the open and closed reserve sections; the range of resources in the audio-visual section; how to reserve materials currently out on loan; and how to arrange access to materials held in other libraries through inter-library loans. These are just a few of the many library functions which the serious student will want to know about and be able to use.

Stephen, a university honours student in social sciences, found that his initial trip through the library at the commencement of first year was just an introduction. He actually participated in the tour several times over the following years to refresh his mind and revitalise his skills. At the start of his honours year, the expectations about his research work were much higher. He had to organise a computer search of the relevant literature held in an American database. He found the process to be both challenging, and frankly, amazing. He sat with a staff member and used the computer to interrogate the database half a world away. The process yielded an abundant supply of articles to be analysed for his thesis.

In summary, whether you are a first or latter year student, you will want to know the geography of your library. Be certain to participate in the orientation program and take at least one tour of your library. Your goal is to be able to walk into the library with specific research questions and to find the answers quickly and efficiently. Knowing the various departments and their functions will help you to fulfil these tasks.

Saving time in the library

As suggested earlier, the library can absorb alot of student time. Students who are not sufficiently familiar with the geography and functions of the various sections are most vulnerable to wasting time in fruitless searches. Here are some pointers to help make your library visits more efficient and effective.

- List your specific research goals for each trip to the library plus an expected completion time. Aim to complete your search by the prescribed time.
- Try to use the library facilities at off-peak times to minimise waiting in queues.
- Prior to arriving at the library, make a comprehensive list of topics which need researching. Try to minimise return trips just to tie up loose ends.
- If you are unfamiliar with the research topic, ask a librarian for advice about general resources, such as annual reviews or topical yearbooks.
- Avoid garrulous classmates while conducting your library research. Socialising is best left to your leisure time.
- Before going to the bookshelves to look for your reference

sources, check the loan list to see which books are unavailable.

- For books you deem to be crucial and which are out on loan, place an urgent recall request with the circulation librarian.
- When queues are long at the photocopier or circulation desk, come back later or start reading the reference material while standing and waiting.
- Use efficient reading techniques to skim and scan for pertinent resource material. Ask yourself while scanning whether this is useful. If so, how?
- Be sparing in your note-taking as notes are time-consuming. When taking notes, be brief and concise—get the important nouns, forget prepositions and articles.
- When recording a note, be sure to indicate where you think the note can be used in your assignment. Students are frequently mystified when they later read some library research notes, wondering why they ever took the notes in the first place.
- Get to know your classmates so that you can share resources. It is far more economical on everyone's time if you can arrange to work as a syndicate on major projects. One person can make the trip to the library and photocopy relevant material for distribution to syndicate members.
- When searching for books and materials which are hard to get, contact other local libraries or consider arranging an inter-library loan.
- Use the telephone before making a trip to the library to enquire about the availability of resources difficult to find.

As you see from the above list of pointers, some of them involve working with classmates to achieve a positive group result. Generally, several heads are better than one. This is particularly so when time is at a premium and resources are scarce. So, band together and work towards mutually beneficial and positive results.

If a group cannot be formed, then an alternative approach may help. James was a third-year engineering student who had previously been doing his course part-time. In order to complete his degree more quickly, he returned to university full-time for his third year. However, he occasionally worked for his previous employer, a civil engineering/management consultancy firm, on a casual basis during holiday periods.

Prior to the mid-year break, James requested the syllabus for the research subject he would be doing in second semester. He noted the suggested topics and discussed the possibilities with two of the firm's engineers. Based on their advice and the availability of the firm's research resources, he chose a project topic which could be pursued at the office before and after work. He found the consultants at the firm to be very helpful and he had access to the computer equipment to search various databases and library holdings. When James returned to university for the second semester, he was already well on his way with the research project.

The message in the preceding case study is: use all available resources to pursue your goals. By looking ahead and planning wisely, James was able to reduce some of the academic pressure during second semester. He was also able to benefit from the alternative information sources available through his firm.

General principles for efficient assignment research

Most students will have many research assignments to complete during their academic years. While the library will be the central focus for much of your work, there are some planning principles which will make you more efficient and your research more effective.

- As soon as you receive the assignment, get started straight-away. Don't procrastinate!
- When in doubt about the interpretation of the research topic, clarify it with your instructor.
- Set up a chart and assign weekly goals for researching and writing.
- Establish a preliminary outline so that your early reading and note-taking is targeted to a specific section of the project.
- List your research goals before entering the library.
- Use the library at off-peak times to avoid crowds and queues.
- If you are uncertain about where to start your library research, ask a librarian.

- Be certain you keep abreast of new research equipment at the library. Learn new researching skills when the opportunity arises.
- Share resources with other students.
- Be certain to set firm deadlines for completing your library research.
- Accept the fact that you will never know everything about the topic you are researching, unless it happens to be an autobiographical project. Resist the temptation to put off starting your writing until you know 'just a little more'.
- Start writing your first draft on the predetermined date. To complete your drafting and rewriting, you will need plenty of time.

Summary

Using your library well and keeping up to date with your researching skills will save you time and increase the quality of your research papers. The prime secrets are to be disciplined and determined. Get to work straightaway and work to predetermined weekly goals. The most important goal to respect is 'Start Writing Day!' If at any time along the way confusion arises, be certain to get help. Librarians are very helpful people. Asking a few specific questions can often clarify confusion and produce relevant research information.

Practical exercises

1 Approach your teaching staff and the Readers' Assistance Librarian at your library and suggest the possibility of structuring several simulated research exercises which you and your classmates could carry out. The exercises could be planned so that you have to use most of the common research tools available in your library to complete the project.

2 In conjunction with several classmates and perhaps a teaching staff member, construct a list of relevant research databases or other information sources which might be tapped by students in your subject area.

3 Volunteer for appropriate training so you can help the library staff conduct the library tours at the beginning of the academic year. As the saying goes, the best way to learn a subject is to teach it.

7
Writing essays

- Establish a file
- Plan the project
- Set weekly goals
- Preliminary reading
- Tentative outline
- Researching and note-taking
- Writing the first draft
- Redrafting
- Learning from your marked essays
- Practical exercises

It's Friday of Week Ten and you have several assignments due in the next fortnight. What is particularly concerning is that you have been studiously ignoring the large assignment in your most difficult subject. To just think about the preliminary reading for this assignment causes heart palpitations, but it *is* due next Monday. That leaves just the weekend to get it done.

Long days of reading and longer nights of writing. The friend you had hoped would be available to type the paper is away for the weekend, so it's going to be hand-written. As the hours press onwards, your handwriting gets less legible. It's Sunday evening now and your mind is spinning and your hand is hurting. Negative thoughts plague you—'This is really a royal load of rubbish!' As you read various sections of the paper, you begin to agree with that statement. What you're trying to say doesn't really make much sense, and, there's no time for redrafting. Maybe the marker will see some flicker of enlightenment?? Wishful thinking. The paper gets finished, but in the early hours of Monday morning. You stagger into the classroom bleary eyed and weary minded and hope for the best. You tell yourself that you'll get started earlier on the next paper. But, didn't I say that after the last paper as well?

I hope that scenario does not apply to your writing habits. But, on a probability basis, if procrastination is not a problem for you, it certainly will be for many of your classmates. Procrastination is very prevalent and almost endemic amongst student populations. Why? Probably because thorough research and good writing take time and effort and *hard work*. The problem is not really laziness but more so, fear—fear of not succeeding in the task. 'This is a tough essay topic and I haven't a clue about the area. Maybe inspiration will strike me tomorrow.' But, we all know tomorrow never comes; it's just a comforting excuse for avoiding the pain of writing.

This chapter is all about writing and how to deal with the procrastination problem. The sections describe a method by which you can get started and keep moving on your essays and reports. In essence, there are a series of steps you can use to make the writing process more productive and far less threatening. That last word might sound ominous, but putting ideas down onto paper for evaluation is a threatening process for many students. However, with practice, patience and perseverance your confidence will increase and the threat will become progressively less severe.

Establish a file for each assignment

The first job to carry out when you are given a writing assignment is to establish a file. A Manila folder is perfectly suitable and quite cheap. Label the folder with the project name and due date and then spend a few minutes thinking about the topic.

Record your early thoughts and ideas even though you might think that on Day One of the project you know absolutely nothing about the assigned topic. Perhaps, but you may have intuitions and 'gut responses'. Don't worry at this stage about quality, just record any ideas and reactions which pop into your mind about the topic. You might be surprised later on at the relevance of some of these thoughts.

In order to guide your early thinking, highlight or underline in red ink the key terms which appear in the assignment topic. Having underlined these terms, ask yourself how the terms relate to each other. You might also want to consider broader perspectives, such as how these terms relate to the key objectives of the subject and course for which the assignment is being written. Generally, any early thoughts can be helpful in getting you started.

Plan the project

Five minutes of planning will save you hours of time. That truism is particularly relevant when preparing and writing large assignments.

Josie was a mature age post-graduate student who had written many essays in her academic career. But she had never written a 50 000 word thesis. She consulted me after her first meeting with her supervisor when she seriously questioned whether she was capable of managing her thesis. We discussed her ideas and then possible ways of dividing the thesis topics into chapters. At this early stage, she could specify with some coaxing six chapters which would cover the thesis subject quite well. We then selected the easiest chapter and divided it into four sections. When asked how many paragraphs she thought she would need to cover any particular section, she said about twenty to thirty. Twenty or so paragraphs sounded manageable and Josie was willing to get started. Her attitude seemed far more positive when leaving my office than when she entered.

That single planning session not only helped Josie organise her approach, it also boosted her confidence. She continued to see me on an occasional basis when her confidence flagged, but I'm happy to report that she completed her thesis in minimum time and with a very positive result. After the thesis was done, Josie said that focusing upon paragraphs rather than the whole was her salvation. Metaphorically speaking, she could see herself conquering each next step, but had she focused upon the entire trip, she might well have fallen along the way and not resumed the journey.

Set weekly goals

Let's assume your project is not a major thesis, but a routine essay. As most students are expected to write essays of 1000–3000 words with perhaps four to six weeks of preparation time, let's choose as an example an essay of 3000 words to be completed in five weeks. In order to schedule your tasks, establish some weekly goals such as the following.

Week 1: Establish folder; record early thoughts, reactions and approaches to topic; if confused, clarify topic with teaching staff; write a preliminary outline; commence initial reading and note-taking.

Week 2: Continue reading and note-taking; if difficulties finding appropriate resources, consult library staff; refine outline.

Week 3: Further reading and note-taking; discuss topic and outline with friends to sharpen your understanding of the issues.

Week 4: Finalise outline; tidy up any outstanding reading or note-taking matters; *start writing on   /   /   !!*

Week 5: Finish first draft; redraft daily, at least three or four times; have a friend read a draft for their comments; correct typographical errors; submit on time.

Having specified various weekly goals, let's look at some of these activities in more detail.

Clarify the topic

Any experienced teacher will confirm the frequency with which students misread or wrongly interpret assigned essay topics. Regrettably, some very fine essays are submitted, but on tangential or completely inappropriate subjects. Instead of directing their attention to the nub of the matter, some students stray from the central theme at the very outset and never really get back on target. Can high marks be earned for an essay written essentially on the wrong topic? No.

If you are in doubt about any aspect of the assignment, then clarify the matter straightaway. Most teaching staff are quite happy to take a few minutes to discuss interpretation issues relating to assignment topics. Of course they will not go so far as to structure an outline for you—that's your responsibility. The important point to bear in mind is that teaching staff do not think students are dumb when they seek to clarify a point of potential confusion—especially if the student shows evidence of some basic thinking and reading about the topic.

Write a preliminary outline

Having established your file and done some initial thinking about the topic, take pen in hand and jot down a preliminary outline. You might think that this step is premature. It's not. Even a very general outline will help to organise your thinking. The outline might be as general as: Introduction 1, 2, 3; Body 1, 2, 3; Summary/Conclusion 1, 2, 3. The numbers following the headings stand for points, ideas or concepts which will be developed. At the preliminary stage, just put some initial ideas down. They can be changed as you become more informed about the essay topic.

Initial reading

If you know something about the topic, then you are off to a running start. However, it is very likely you will have to write essays on topics about which you know absolutely nothing.

When this is the case, you will profit by doing some background reading. Your library will probably have a range of books and reference sources which can give you a brief overview before you get down to more specific reading. Some reference sources which might be helpful include the encyclopaedias, yearbooks and world books, almanacs, and review editions of specific journals. Your librarians will be able to suggest some other general background reading to familiarise you with your topic.

Note-taking

Note-taking is a critical step in researching—it is your record of information gleaned from various sources. You will ultimately want to mix, shuffle and recombine these notes to make a tight and convincing argument. Having written many essays, papers, and books, I wish to recommend the use of note cards as the recording medium. You can purchase note cards at any stationery shop. Lined cards which are about 75 × 120mm will be adequate for most note-taking purposes. They are slightly more expensive than tablet paper, but they are more resilient and more easily carried and dealt into topical piles during the writing stage.

I have found the best way to use the note cards is to write the bibliographic details on one side of the card and various notes on the reverse side. There are several different types of notes to make. Firstly, write a note to yourself about where in the essay you think the note belongs. You can use the letters and numbers referred to earlier, such as Intro 2 or B 3 to signify second point in the introduction and third issue in the body. In addition to the letters and numbers, you might want to add a further few words, but keep it brief. For example, 'B 2: historical point, justifies major argument' will help you to remember where and how you intended to use the information at the drafting stage.

The actual note or summary you make from the reference source should be preferably in your own words. No essay marker will want to read a collection of direct quotations from various learned scholars. The marker wants to know what *you* think of the writings of these persons. It is an exercise of finding pertinent resource information and then critically assessing it. Your essay is then the medium by which the thoughts of others are critically evaluated. One hopes the essay draws valid conclusions based upon sound evidence. Therefore, ask yourself during the reading of a potentially relevant reference source whether it is relevant. If so, how? But, write your thoughts in your own words; do not copy verbatim from the reference sources.

Many students feel insecure when they are doing reference reading and therefore take far too many notes. In the early stages of researching, you will probably think that just about everything you read is pertinent to the topic. However, as you become more informed, some of the points you previously thought were relevant are now seen to be tangential or even inapplicable. That is the benefit of doing some preliminary reading to obtain an overview. If you can not specify exactly where a note will fit in your existing outline, either change the outline (you will have to convince yourself that the change is worthwhile and justifiable) or pass on to other more relevant note sources. Remember, note-taking is time-consuming. There is absolutely no benefit in taking notes which ultimately you will not use in the essay.

Since you will be spending considerable time pursuing references, mostly in the library, consult the previous chapter about library researching skills. One pointer will save you much time: plan your library research visits before you arrive. List the references you want to locate for reading. Having organised your search, you will avoid the aimless wanderings which many students pursue in the stacks of their library.

Other preparations

Having progressed into the research phase, it might be helpful to test your understanding of the topic and your treatment of the issues by discussing the project with a friend. Simply ask a friend to sit and listen while you present a five-minute overview of the essay topic. Include in this presentation your line of argument and how you are developing the central ideas. If you have progressed to the point of conclusions, include them as well. This presentation is a test case and is likely to bring to your mind or to the mind of your friend any glaring oversights or fundamental errors in argument. The small amount of time taken in this mini-presentation is well worthwhile.

Prior to the drafting stage, reconsider your outline and make any relevant changes. These changes might come from your recent research, your thinking, or from the comments of your friend following the presentation just suggested.

Writing the first draft

The most difficult day of any writing project is the first day of drafting. It is perfectly predictable that you will be feeling insecure and inadequate about your knowledge of the topic. These strong feelings will most likely tempt you to put off the writing until you check just a few more references. However, assuming that you have been working steadily from the very beginning of the project, it is crucial that you *start writing on the scheduled day*. You will have to admit to yourself that there will always be some other references to be read, but time for writing is more important.

The best way to get into the writing is to sort through your note cards and place them into stacks under relevant headings. The note cards are ideal for this function. Having distributed the cards into their relevant stacks, decide where you want to start. If your paper is reasonably short, then the beginning is the logical place. However, for longer papers, you might want to consider starting on the easiest part. In laboratory reports, the method section is very straightforward and easy to write. The practical suggestion is to start where you can build some momentum quickly and easily.

Word processors are becoming increasingly more popular with students. One of the best investments you can make is to purchase a personal computer and then learn ten-finger typing. You can purchase or borrow typing tutor software packages which make learning to type interesting. Ten minutes a day of practice will get you up to a functional speed inside of two or three months.

When is the best time of the day to do the writing? Depends on the individual, but try to find a period when you can be free from distractions. I've found early morning to be very good. I have never been disturbed by phone calls at 5.00 am. You might say that you're too sleepy at that time, but a brisk run or walk or some energetic callisthenics for 30 minutes will shake you into wakefulness and stimulate your mind for clear and logical thinking.

Writing is difficult and many people find they need a prolonged warming-up period to really get moving. If this applies to you, plan for longer writing periods, perhaps in the order of two or three hours to make any real headway on the project. To maximise your output, arrange for a quiet and distraction-free writing period. Having become settled, specify *in writing* a goal for that writing period. Write the goal in your diary or on a planning sheet so that it becomes a contract between you and the project. Remember, people who work to written goals are much more likely to accomplish them. And following on from that, accomplishing your first goal is the best way of preparing for the second.

If you get blocked along the way, and it happens to virtually every writer at some stage, try this anti-blocking strategy. Move away from your desk and sit in a comfortable chair. Close your eyes and take a few easy breaths. Say 'R-e-l-a-x-x' as you breathe out. When comfortable and relaxed both in mind and body, visualise the immediately preceding points and let them float in your mind. If you know where your argument is going, then float those ideas in your mind as well. Having floated the befores and afters, you now want your mind to generate the in-betweens, the ideas which will connect the two.

The mechanics of this process are not really understood, but they do draw on what we call the subconscious. No matter what the mechanism might be, I've found that the process works about three out of four times. I come out of this peaceful trance-like state with several ideas which allow the writing process to progress. Some of the ideas may be changed or adapted later, but the immediate benefit is that the block is broken.

Another technique is to draw a rectangle and write inside it a few words about the issue which is blocking you. Then relax as described above and when relaxed see if you can write four points to be attached to each of the corners of the rectangle. It is surprising how your mind when relaxed can generate three or four related points to the blocked topic. Some of these points can possibly be used in the essay to get over the blocked area.

Redrafting and polishing

'Good writing is good rewriting', so the saying goes. Unfortunately, many students who have procrastinated and started too late for redrafting end up submitting their first draft, which is generally far short of a polished product. The best redrafting approach is to finish your first draft and then re-read the work on several succeeding days. You are a slightly different person on each of these occasions and you will undoubtedly see revision possibilities.

On the other hand, a friend can provide useful insights as well. You will have had that essay bouncing around inside your head for not only several days, but also, one hopes, several weeks. Given the amount of time taken and energy used, it is very likely that the words you have written have almost become part of you. With that intense level of familiarity, is it possible that you can be an objective and critical judge? No, not generally. Seasoned writers know that they can misread blatant errors in their own writing because they are too familiar with the text. Your appointed reader is not.

The best time for your friend to read your essay is two days before it is due for submission. If some major sources of concern emerge, which means that your friend finds errors in content or syntax in addition to the occasional typographic mistake, then you still have time to make any necessary corrections. If your work has been prepared on a word processor, the editing is relatively painless. Trying to delete and/or add paragraphs in a handwritten essay can look messy and give the marker a very poor initial impression.

Submitting your essay

There might be specific instructions about the form in which your essay is to be submitted. You might need to purchase a special folder or binder. Plan ahead and have the necessary equipment. You will almost certainly have specifications about how to identify your work, whether it be by your name or student number. Be certain that these details are adhered to exactly.

Deliver your essay in person to the correct staff member. As essays are one of the major contributors to your final mark, it is best to deliver your work in person. Treat your essay like a bank cheque for one million dollars. Would you give such a cheque to a classmate for depositing? Generally, no.

Even though members of the teaching staff are almost infallible, occasionally things go wrong. There have been reports of students who have delivered their essay on the due date to the correct member of staff, but somehow the essay became lost prior to the marking. Probably the best method to ensure a fail-safe submission is to request a receipt from the person to whom the essay is submitted. This might appear slightly paranoid, unless of course you are one of the students who has had an essay or two go missing after submission.

Extensions

Inspite of previously impeccable health and robust fitness, the blessed flu or other maladies can knock you flat, especially when you can least afford the time. There can be other sources of distress, such as the illness or death of a family member, a serious accident, or even litigation and court appearances. All of these events are very distressing and of sufficient impact to erode the concentration of most students. If your essay preparation has been affected by any untoward event, be certain to obtain appropriate documentation. The assumption will be made by the administration that if the event was of sufficient emotional or physical importance to impede your researching or writing, then it would be appropriate for you to seek relevant professional help or advice. Be certain to obtain a letter or certificate stating the dates and general nature of the situation which impeded your progress. Keep a copy of all documents and submit the originals with a covering letter specifying the relevant details to your course administrator.

Learning from your marked essays

Many students receiving their marked essays look immediately at the mark and then perhaps at any comments in the margins. There might be tears of joy or sorrow, but chances are the mark reflects the degree of understanding and the level of preparation which went into the project. That evening most students will file the essay in a folder and probably never look at it again. A few will toss it in the rubbish can. Regrettably, all of these students are ignoring a most valuable and potent educational resource.

What can you do with your marked essays? Firstly, read through the entire essay and take careful note of any corrections and comments. We are creatures of habit and given a free hand, we are very likely to repeat the same errors time and time again. One of the functions of most educational institutions is to break this habit and interject a new, more correct way of thinking and performing.

A few words to the teaching staff who are reading this chapter. Psychological studies have shown convincingly that positive reinforcement far surpasses punitive measures when new behaviours are being learned. If you want to increase the learning potential of your students, be sure to acknowledge the positive points in their essays. Nothing is more frustrating for students than to receive a 'marked' essay which contains only a number or letter, but no comments or suggestions. In addition to specifying criticisms, bend over backwards to find something positive to say which will be encouraging to the essay writer.

Learning from the marked essays of classmates

A final note about an ancillary learning resource—the marked essays of your classmates. Even if you failed in your essay, try to see your paper as a learning medium. By understanding your errors, you can improve next time. The best way to gain an appreciation of what is a good essay in the eyes of your teacher is to locate a paper with a high mark.

Try to locate one or two classmates who scored well on their essays and ask if you could read their work. Study their writing style and the structure of their argument. What sources did they use to justify their argument? What about citing evidence and references? Were their paragraphs well structured with variety in sentence length and style? How did they convince the marker that they knew what they were talking about? These are but a few questions which might produce some interesting and educational insights for you. If you are not overstepping your welcome, speak with the writers of these highly marked essays and try to obtain an understanding of how they developed their skills. You are surrounded in class by learning possibilities, so take every opportunity to learn from them.

Practical exercises

Essay writing requires a complicated set of skills, but practice will help considerably. Most students wait for the two or three major essays in each subject to obtain this practice. It's far better to practise beforehand when the marking will not count. Here are some suggestions to improve your writing skills.

1   Ask one of the more approachable teachers you know if you could submit to him/her a one-page mini-essay twice a week. Such a brief piece of work would only take five minutes at most to read and mark. Choose a short article to read and analyse, and then write a critical summary in one page. If you do this twice a week for a semester or two, you *will* increase your writing skills. Your progress will be accelerated by the twice-weekly feedback you obtain from the marking teacher.

2   When reading your textbooks and reference sources, analyse the writing style of the author. How was the topic developed? What evidence was utilised? How were the sentences being structured? Enquiring minds produce educating answers.

3   Join the writers' society on your campus or offer to write some articles for the student newspaper. During your 'apprenticeship', learn from the more experienced writers in the group.

4   Write letters to distant friends, especially those who make you feel good. You don't necessarily need to receive responses, but if you do, that's a bonus. See your letters as short stories or analyses of your current life. Every writing task you complete is valuable experience.

8
Revision skills

- Planning your revision campaign
- Getting help when needed
- Learning on the run
- Practical exercises

Vickie had just finished formal classes at the end of her first year of a social work degree. She was now facing her first set of university examinations. During the academic year, Vickie had made a valiant effort at keeping pace with her four subjects, but occasionally fell behind. In spite of her hard work, Vickie's assignments teetered on the pass/fail margin, with an average result of 53 per cent. The final exams were worth 60 per cent of her final mark—so the pressure was really on.

On her first 'stu vac' revision day, she opened her folders containing her year's notes and looked over some of the pages. The notes in one subject looked like ancient Greek (not one of her subjects). She immediately thought, I'm going to *fail!* She became intensely nervous. Vickie's breathing became rapid and shallow. Her hands and knees began to quiver. Before she knew it, she was experiencing a full-blown panic attack.

Perhaps some aspects of that scenario are applicable to your preparation periods prior to examinations. There's no doubt about it, exams produce anxiety and possibly panic—unless of course you know all of the answers.

But, how do you overcome the trauma and anxiety of examinations? There are two words which hold the answer to exam woes. What do you think they are? Every boy scout and Trivial Pursuit enthusiast should know them ... *be prepared!!* Yes, that's easily said, but much more difficult to do. Why? Generally, because being well prepared for examinations requires diligent and disciplined study—hard work. To make matters even more difficult, this hard work is best applied right from day one of the course—a time when few students want to dedicate time to examination preparation, especially if their exams are nine months away.

To counter all of this talk about hard work, which is an inevitable part of positive exam preparation, let me quickly add a promising note. Your hard work will be made far less onerous and threatening if you start the preparation early. This chapter will describe some of the ways in which you can organise your revision and gain the maximum marks in your exams.

Lecture revision

As stated in the chapter on note-taking, the process of taking good lecture notes starts before the actual lecture. Five to ten minutes of browsing through a relevant chapter will 'oil your mental gears' and contribute to a better set of notes. If you arrive early for your lecture, then spend a few minutes revising the notes from the last lecture in that subject. These warming-up activities are very important preliminary stages in the longer term learning process.

Probably the most critical first revision is just after each lecture. At this point, the topics should be fresh in your mind. If time permits and no other classes are scheduled for the following hour, either stay seated in the lecture hall or move to the library. Read through your notes and make any additions or corrections which you think are necessary. If you are confused about any topic, then consult your text or other references and make supplementary notes. You can tape ancillary notes onto the borders of your class notes to produce a more comprehensive account.

Many students, especially those for whom English is a second language, tape-record all of their lectures. This is done primarily because of their uncertainty about their language skills, particularly their ability to understand and to get down into note form all of the essential information presented during lectures. They play the tapes and check their notes, but frequently stop, rewind and then replay parts of the lecture to make necessary adjustments to their notes. The whole process can take a surprising amount of time. On average, it will take well over one hour to replay a 50-minute lecture. The best approach is to train yourself to become a more efficient note-taker. There are recommended practical exercises at the end of Chapter 2 which might be of help.

If you have made tapes of previous lectures, then there is absolutely no harm in replaying them, but try to do this at non-peak study times. Ideal opportunities for these replays are when you're walking, shopping, cleaning or driving. These are times when it would be difficult, if not impossible to write, read, or solve problems. Students who revise 'on the run' benefit in two ways: they have more opportunities for working their way through their notes and study materials; and they are increasing their time management and personal efficiency skills.

Weekend learning

One of the most practical and beneficial steps to increase your learning potential and to maximise your marks is to revise each weekend. Sounds like a fun killer, but revision is a necessity and the research on learning methods is crystal clear—regular and spaced learning is far, far superior to last-minute cramming.

I would be naive to say, 'Forget about cramming'. It's a time-honoured student tradition. Just about every student has found that cramming is necessary at some stage of their academic career. Even those who are very well prepared usually spend that last night before their exams doing a bit of frantic revising. Inspite of this tendency, get the whole process into gear early in the year and learn as you go.

If your weekends tend to follow a set routine, try to find a three-hour period which you can dedicate solely to revision. That time is not to be used for writing essays, preparing lab reports or doing research reading. It is to be used only for revising, that is *learning* your notes and other materials. Pull out the lecture notes and any other resources which have been generated during the last week. Go through these notes very carefully, learning them as if you had an examination on the topics Monday morning at 9.00 am.

I can hear the deafening chorus of moans and groans. Yes, isolating yourself on a sunny weekend morning to learn your notes is not exactly a fun time recipe. No one ever said that all learning experiences will be joyous occasions. It *is* hard work, but the product of that weekend work will be surprising. Not only will you be significantly decreasing the pre-exam stress, but you will also be gaining a far greater understanding of the concepts as you progress through each subject. The topics covered in Week Two become part of your working knowledge for Week Three and for the rest of the semester and year. Most of your colleagues will not discover and master these topics until they retrieve their notes from those dusty folders just prior to their exams.

Revision for quizzes and tests

Your teaching staff are very aware of the difficulties in motivating students to learn progressively through the course. Therefore, they schedule periodic quizzes and tests to coerce you to study and to break any tendency to procrastinate. Here are some helpful suggestions to bear in mind when revising for these assessment exercises.

- Consult your syllabus and take special note of any comments made about assessments. Note particularly the different types of quizzes, tests and examinations which are scheduled (or those which may be administered without prior warning). Ask whether there may be multiple-choice sections and/or short answer questions; mathematical problems; and major essay questions.
- If your syllabus does not specify the types of test and examination questions which you are likely to get, then speak with former students who studied your subjects last year. They will most likely be able to tell you what to expect and how to prepare for the assessments.
- Plan for sufficient time to revise your lecture notes and other resources at least four to five times. Repetition is a great teacher, but repetition takes a lot of time!
- As you revise each lecture, ask yourself what are the three most examinable topics in this lecture. Note them briefly on a separate sheet for later consideration.
- Meet with a classmate whose ability and commitment you respect and compare notes on these highly examinable topics. Discuss the topics you noted in common.
- Remember, a good examiner will expect you to know well any basic course topics A, B, and C. Particularly probing examiners will go beyond just memorised definitions and will ask about relationship issues, A–B, B–C and A–C.
- Superior students will not only know about these critical relationships, but also about their implications and the assumptions upon which they are based.

Early morning revision on exam day

Most of the revision which has been recommended above pertains to the months, weeks and days prior to assessments. Many students have asked whether they risk burnout if they study too much just before their examinations. The answer is generally, no.

If you have been preparing and revising on a daily and weekly basis, then the assessments pose only a polishing problem. Imagine that it's the night before a test and you have completed your revision. Should you get up early and run through the material again? Yes. Assuming that you have allowed sufficient time for some good sleep, an early morning revision will help to get your mind primed and 'prepped' for the assessment. That early morning session should be just a light scan of the notes. It certainly is not a time to confront a new and complex topic which you suddenly think is prime exam material.

Revising at the exam venue

Visit any campus during the examination period and you will find groups of tense students gathered at the steps of the large lecture halls and other examination sites. You will see small groups of students either debating contentious issues or nervously laughing while trying to distract themselves with chatter about frivolities. The astute students are sitting off to the side and quietly thinking or reading over the major concepts from their notes.

A cautionary note is very relevant here. Let's assume your preparation has not been exactly thorough and that you have been burning too much midnight oil trying to revise your notes for the *first* time. (Horrors!!) You arrive at the exam venue early and start talking with a friend who seems to be sharing your misery. Just then, another classmate rushes up and blurts, 'What did you think about that article by Green and Simmons?' Your mind goes into a whirl ... 'Who the Hell are Green and Simmons??? What did they write about? Have I missed something which is really critical? Will this article be the basis for the major essay? It probably will be. Oh, my God, I'm going to *fail*!!!'

Perhaps that monologue will be very familiar to some of you. All kinds of experiences and thoughts can plague a student's mind during the final hours before an exam. Even though students have equal access to positive and negative thoughts, they seem to gravitate to the latter on exam days. In order to keep calm and maintain rational thinking during this critical period, stay removed from your classmates. By all means, avoid the gloom and doom squad, devious manipulators or obnoxious know-it-alls. Hide in the bushes if you must, or better yet, find a nearby classroom and sit quietly alone.

In the exam room: the last-ditch opportunity

Once you have entered the examination room, you will not be permitted to consult your notes, unless you are sitting for an open-book exam. However, your mind will still be capable of pondering any special points which might be lingering delicately on the brink of a cortical crevasse. You have the ability to exercise active recall or loose the idea in a fogbound abyss. (If the latter occurs, there are still means of rescuing these ideas. Read the section on mental blocking on page 125.)

After the exam papers have been distributed and you have been given the 'go ahead' signal, jot down quickly any notes which you think might break away from the cortical edge and plummet into darkness. Having noted these points, you can then proceed with a calmer mind.

End of year exam revision

The end of year exams are major events in the academic life of most students. As suggested earlier, these exams will have been noted and scheduled in the subject syllabus. In spite of this warning, most students will actively repress the inevitability of these exams, mostly because of the associated anxiety. Repression and denial become strongly developed by the time students reach upper secondary or tertiary levels. Hence, the tradition of cramming.

In order to do full justice to your final exams, you will really need to schedule your revisions over a six-week period. Yes, that is also the time when many essays, reports, and other assessable projects are due, but examinations will count for the majority of your final marks. Thus, it is best to allocate your time in proportion to the distribution of these marks. If tests, essays and reports are worth 40 per cent and your final exam is worth 60, then be sure your preparation time correctly reflects this ratio.

As suggested earlier, learning anything well will take mutiple repetitions. The number five is a conservative index to guide your revision planning. That means trying to organise the six weeks before your exams so that you can read over and *learn* your notes five times. That might sound impossible or unappealing or both, but revision and learning *are* functions of repetition.

You might want to chart the revision period and post it in a prominent place where you can easily see it.

6 Week Revision Plan

Subjects	Weeks					
	1	2	3	4	5	6
A	Rev'n 1		Rev'n 2	Rev'n 3	Rev'n 4	Rev'n 5
B	R1	R2	R3	R4	R5	
C		R1		R2	R3	R4 R5
D			R1		R2	R3 R4

Note: R = Revision

From this chart, you will see that different subjects require different revision times. In scheduling your revision periods, choose times when you are fresh and alert. Remember, you can revise 'on the run' by carrying flash cards or other materials for use on buses and trains and while standing in a queue. Try to focus your revision on topics which you believe to be highly examinable. If you strike difficulties, contact a person who can explain the topic(s) to you.

Summary

Revising for your exams is best done from the early weeks of the semester. Revise your class notes within 24 hours of each lecture and then learn them in a dedicated revision session each Saturday or Sunday morning. When going through your notes, try to anticipate highly examinable topics. Make a list of these items and then compare your list with the topics gleaned by several classmates. Be certain to start your revision for your final exams sufficiently early to allow for many (five or more) repetitions through your notes. The crucial motto for good exam candidates: be prepared!

Practical exercises

1 Prepare a schedule for the weekends during the present semester and include a dedicated three-hour period at the same time each weekend for *exam revision*. Give that time period high priority. It will win you many marks in the final exams.
2 Organise a weekly lunch meeting with two or three committed classmates in your most difficult subject. Agree to discuss/revise the examinable topics raised in the lectures over the past week.
3 Prepare a revision chart for the six weeks preceding your final exam period.
4 Revise your lecture notes and other materials and write a list of the three most examinable topics from each lecture or reading assignment.

9
Dealing with academic and exam anxiety

- Academic anxiety—thinking more positively
- Participating in classroom discussions
- Learning how to relax and function better
- Reducing exam anxiety
- Practical exercises

You might be surprised to learn that post-graduate students and medical doctors are not immune from exam anxiety. Carl, a doctor referred by the chief surgeon at his hospital, had failed his surgical fellowship exams several times. With each failure, he became increasingly anxious about whether he would pass at the next set of exams. His particular worry was the viva exam, a particularly difficult assessment which required candidates to interview patients and then be examined by two doctors. Carl's anxiety about his viva exams was so extreme that it began to adversely affect his daily life and professional practice.

Carl's hands were damp, verging on wet with perspiration when I first met him. He reported that at 39 years of age with a large family to support, he was faced with the very real and negative prospect of failing in his career. If he failed his fifth attempt at the viva exams, he was prepared to leave medicine altogether and look for a business opportunity elsewhere. He stated quite firmly that if he could not practise as a surgeon, he would not work in medicine at all.

With so much experience and knowledge (the Chief of Surgery who referred him said he was very knowledgeable, but just pathologically anxious about the viva exams), I thought it would be a true loss if he were not able to get through that next examination. To that end, we started a relaxation and desensitisation series (more about this later) and also discussed ways in which he could make his revision more efficient and effective. With a major assault on his books and notes and many practice sessions of relaxation training, I am happy to say that Carl passed his vivas and is now practising as a fully qualified and very satisfied surgeon.

In addition to examination anxiety which almost curtailed Carl's career, this chapter will deal with academic anxiety, a common difficulty for many students who panic at the mere thought of speaking in class or getting down to effective work on a difficult assignment. As the latter is more prevalent, let's start there first.

Academic anxiety

Academic anxiety can be described as grit in your mental gears. That high-performance machine within your cranium is fuelled and fired up, but grit in the gears can grind down your performance. Metaphorically speaking, the grit causes negative versus positive thoughts. Fears of failure or of low performance cause you to become reticent in certain academic situations. For example, getting started on major projects and speaking in class are some of the most common problems experienced by students.

Jennifer was a secretary for five years before deciding to go to technical college to obtain her HSC as an entry qualification for a university degree in marketing. Even though she was a very efficient secretary and a highly organised housekeeper, she still felt very nervous about undertaking serious study. She was an avid reader, yet she claimed her mind wandered off target. Her boss had previously given her considerable responsibility in drafting letters and reports, but when working on an essay, she would sit and wait and wait before generating sufficient courage (panic?) to get herself moving.

Jennifer seemed to think that her reading and writing skills were deficient because 'it's been so many years since I've studied'. She also compared herself unfavourably to her younger classmates whom she saw as brimming with confidence and up-to-date competence in their subject areas. These feelings ultimately progressed beyond the metaphorical grit in her gears to a full stop and an inability to restart. Fortunately, Jennifer had sufficient life experience to know that most problems have at least one solution and she sought appropriate help.

Anxiety and fear of failure

Academic anxiety is almost always due to negative thoughts, especially about the possibility of failure or poor performance. Let's look at speaking in the classroom for example. It would be safe to say that few if any classrooms hold any life-threatening risks, yet many students experience feelings of high anxiety when sitting in their classes. These feelings are fundamentally attributable to negative thoughts. If these thoughts can be turned around to become either neutral or better yet, positive, then the student can sit more comfortably in class and learn.

We might look at the anxiety situation as an A, B, C cycle where A represents a negative thought, for example, 'What if I can't answer a question correctly?'; B for nervous feelings; and C, for avoidance of the threatening activity—sitting very quietly and inconspicuously in class. As the whole system hinges upon A, that's the best place to start in dealing with the problem.

If classroom speaking is your Achilles' heel and you choose the back rows in class to minimise the chance of being called upon to speak, then look at the types of thoughts you are entertaining. Yes, you might have had some painful experiences in the past, such as being grossly embarrassed when struck speechless in front of the class while trying to present a report. Or, perhaps a teacher ridiculed you in class because of a particularly poor effort on some project. There's no getting around these situations—they do hurt. But, it is very important for you to note that these are historical events and your present classrooms bear no cause–effect relationship with them. It is directly up to you to influence the present so that these historical events are not repeated.

Acknowledge the painful experience from the past, but then add, 'I am in control of my present behaviour!' It is up to you to take steps to prevent the anxiety from recurring. With thorough preparation for your classes, you can assure yourself that you can handle the classroom situation. You want to put the present situation into a realistic perspective and certainly not allow yourself to emotionally cringe in the shadow of some past event. It will take some practice, but putting into direct action this rational approach to your academic challenges will certainly bear more fruit than defaulting from trying.

The role of being well prepared

As noted above, preparation is very important. Anxiety about classroom participation breeds upon uncertainty. If you know that you are not well prepared for a class, a speech or a project, then it's quite understandable that your mind might be entertaining some catastrophic thoughts about possible embarrassment or failure. The secret is to be well prepared so that you have every possible chance of performing to the best of your ability.

The TUF approach

Getting tough with yourself is often necessary, but that might sound daunting. As an alternative, try the TUF approach, where T, U, F stand for *try, use,* and *fun.*

Instead of putting off things and avoiding threatening but harmless situations, get into the habit of *trying* particular skills every day. If you have had a fear of speaking in class, then practise the skill but in smaller bites. When you arrive in the classroom, make a point of greeting the classmates on either side of you. That's speaking in class, but in a less threatening way. If you know that a topic is going to be discussed tomorrow, then read about the topic tonight and prepare three questions which you might ask in class. It takes less courage to ask a question than to offer an answer. When the opportunity arises, get straight into action and ask one of the relevant questions. You'll be surprised how much easier the task is when you're well prepared and you know what to say. Thus, *try*ing to participate in class is an important step to overcoming anxiety about classroom discussion.

The *use* part of the formula means literally using the skills frequently to increase their strength in your behaviour repertoire. It is well established that skills which are frequently used will strengthen. Those which are ignored and allowed to become idle are likely to weaken and possibly disappear. By using these participation skills most days, you can move from fear to confidence and from hesitation to fluency, a situation which would be very appealing to most students.

Fun is something we all like and it will certainly lubricate your learning. A former teaching colleague, Dick Borkowski, once told me that when faced with teaching a difficult concept, try to turn the learning situation into a game. Games are fun and when students are having fun, they learn much more easily. When trying to increase your classroom speaking skills, look for amusing stories and anecdotes which relate to topics being discussed in class. Practise telling these anecdotes to two or three friends or perhaps several family members. Enjoy the humorous situation and be prepared to laugh, especially at yourself. The principle is to start out in a small way and progress gradually to larger groups.

Learning how to relax

Some people might say that their anxiety level is just too high to ever expect these lighter approaches to have any effect. Whether you are an anxious person or not, relaxation training can produce a very positive result. The following steps should be practised *twice a day* for a period of about three months. After 180 practice sessions or thereabouts, you will have conditioned yourself to respond to the word, 'relax', with a strong and productive relaxation response.

1 Be sure to practise twice daily, especially on busy days—that's when you will need the relaxation and benefit most from its effects.

2 Develop the expectation that you will relax, but don't try too hard. Relaxation is a passive process. In the early practice sessions, your mind will tend to wander off onto other thoughts. Expect this to happen and when it does, just bring your attention back onto the relaxation procedure.

3 Find a quiet setting where you will not be disturbed.

4 Make yourself as comfortable as possible. It's best not to lie down in bed as you are likely to drift off into sleep.

5 Focus upon your breathing. Just breathe comfortably and notice how pleasant it feels to listen to the air flowing in and out.

6 Over the next ten breaths, count to yourself successively from one to ten as you breathe in and say 'Relax' to yourself as you breathe out. If your mind is still quite active and strays from the procedure, then trace the numbers in your palm to fix your mind more strongly onto the relaxation process.

7 Now, concentrate upon the body muscles and move from head down to feet, relaxing the muscles of your body. Simply focus your attention on the following muscle groups and then say, 'Relax'. Feel the tension flowing out and systematically relaxing your body. Start by relaxing your forehead and then move downwards: eyebrows, eyelids, cheeks, mouth, jaws, neck, shoulders, back, upper and then lower arms, chest, abdomen, thighs, calves, ankles and feet.

8 To deepen the relaxation effect, imagine now that you are descending a staircase to a warm and quiet beach. As you

see yourself stepping slowly downwards from step to step, associate the familiar feeling of stepping down one step with a stronger feeling of relaxation. When you reach the bottom of the staircase, see yourself walking out onto the beach and then stretching out on a beach towel. If you have difficulty visualising this scene, ask yourself the following questions. What do I see? (the blue water, the breaking waves, the yellow-white sand, the swaying palms); What do I hear? (the breaking waves, the whistling of the gentle wind in the palm fronds); What do I feel? (the fine texture of the sand, the warmth of the sun); What do I smell? (the salty aroma in the air, the sweet smell of flower blossoms); What do I taste? (the salty taste on my lips). By focusing upon your five senses, you should be able to keep the scene actively in the front of your mind.

9   When fully relaxed, say to yourself: 'I can relax my mind and body. I am in control.'

10   After you have enjoyed the feeling of relaxation for a few minutes, then slowly count from one to five, open your eyes and come back to your previous state of functioning. Stay in the same position and then slowly stretch your arms and legs.

11   You can experience a mini-relaxation effect by briefly pausing any time during your days and taking a comfortably deep breath and then slowly letting the air out while you say 'R-e-l-a-x-x-x' to yourself. To remind yourself to take these brief breaks, place small stickers with a large R on them on your telephone receiver, your car dashboard or at any other place where stress can be a problem.

Reducing exam anxiety

Tony was the youngest of six children in his family. His parents were ambitious for their children and Tony was following in the footsteps of brothers and sisters who had forged very successful careers in medicine, pharmacy, accountancy and optometry. While he had been quite successful in soccer and athletics, his grades in school were only average. He made a Herculean last-ditch effort when studying for his matriculation examination and just scraped into law.

At university, Tony quickly realised that he would have to work much more regularly and systematically, but the examinations plagued him. The high expectations of his parents and the very positive performances of his brothers and sisters placed extreme pressure on Tony. His very competitive nature caused him to experience severe headaches and dizziness prior to his first several examinations. In one exam, he had to leave the room repeatedly because he felt nauseous and feared he would vomit. His doctor found nothing medically wrong with him and referred him to me for treatment of his severe anxiety condition.

Tony started on the relaxation training procedure described above. While he was progressing on the series, I asked Tony to write out several scenes in which he saw himself studying calmly and competently at home, sitting in class, and then writing an examination paper in the same positive manner. The purpose of this exercise was to provide a series of visual stimuli which Tony was to imagine while he was relaxed. He would progressively see himself functioning competently and confidently in the series leading up to the scene in which he visualised himself writing his examination paper. While he progressed through the series, he paired his ever increasing relaxation response with the images of himself in the series of scenes. It has been found through controlled research studies that by pairing the relaxation response to the imagined scenes, it is possible to reduce the anxiety in the real event. Here is a sample of some scenes which might be helpful to you.

Scene one

It is Week One of the year and I am sitting in class. The course coordinator is discussing the syllabus and the various assessment exercises which will determine the final mark. The final exams are nine months away.

Scene two

It is Week Four and I am sitting at home at my desk looking at the schedule of papers, tests and exams which are posted on my planning chart. I note that there are several mid-year exams coming up in about ten weeks.

Scene three

It is Week Seven and I am sitting at my desk preparing for my mid-term exams. I have covered the material thoroughly and feel confident about my preparation.

Scene four

It is the night before my first mid-term exam and I am lying in bed ready to go to sleep. My mind is still buzzing with thoughts about the exam. I start the relaxation series and find myself drifting quickly off to sleep feeling much more calm and confident about my preparation.

Scene five

It is the week before my final exams. I have been obtaining quite good results through the year and I want the same trend to continue into the exams. I am thinking confidently about myself and I am saying, '*I can do it!*'. I feel much more confident about my abilities.

Scene six

It is the day of the first final exam and I awake early after a surpisingly sound sleep. I browse through my notes, knowing that my preparation has been thorough, except for one topic which I will reinforce now. I feel calm and confident.

You will have noticed that the scenes become more positive in orientation. That is what you want to build into your responses so that by the time the final exams arrive, you are feeling calm, confident and in control. I suggest to exam anxious students that they use those three C's (*calm, confident, in control*) as prompters for a positive mental attitude.

In summary, examinations can certainly raise your anxiety level and thus affect your results unless specific steps are taken. By learning the relaxation procedure described in this chapter and coupling with it the desensitisation steps, you can lower your anxiety and increase your marks, by up to 30 per cent! Time and practice are necessary, but that increase in your results makes the small effort well worthwhile.

Practical exercises

1 Take the role of the examiner and write your own examination paper. Examine the syllabus and then write five essay questions which will address the major concepts dealt with in the syllabus. For short answer and multiple-choice questions, write three questions of either style immediately following your revision of the notes from each lecture.

2 Have lunch on a set day each week with a classmate or two and prepare five questions from the last week's notes for your colleagues to answer. They should prepare five questions as well and then exchange questions during your quiz/lunch.

3 If past exam papers are available, revise these well before the examination period and note specifically any similarities in question orientation. Prepare a one-page summary for essay questions which appear in two or more of the past papers.

10
Preparing for specific exams

- Multiple choice
- Short answer
- Essay questions
- Open book
- Laboratory exams
- Auditions
- The medical viva
- Practical exercises

Examinations are firmly entrenched in the academic system, much to the chagrin of most students. Regrettably, just about every subject you will study will conclude with some kind of assessment.

Visualise this end of year scene. You see yourself approaching the gathering of anxious students at the entrance to the examination venue. 'Will X,Y or Z be covered on the exam?? What if a question is asked on topic X? I just dashed through that last night! Do I really understand it?? Not well enough. What if I fail? What an embarrassment!' That frantic, downwardly spiralling monologue is familiar to most students.

As much as you would like to see some new, less anxiety-provoking process replace examinations, I regret to say that examinations are here to stay—at least for the near future. Given that reality, let me offer some encouraging words about how to deal with these assessments. *Preparation* is the key to a more confident and competent approach to these testing ordeals. The more you know about the type of exam you will be confronting, the better you will be able to prepare for it. As will become apparent from the sections of this chapter, different types of exams require different types of preparation. Let's look at some of the varieties of exams which you may well have to confront.

Multiple-choice exams

Multiple-choice exams have become increasingly popular with teaching staff, especially with the advent of very sophisticated computer technology. Optical scanning of answer sheets makes marking a very simple chore. The computer can individually analyse each student's performance and provide question-specific information for follow-up learning. Given the popularity of multiple-choice examinations amongst examiners, it is best to be well informed about what to expect and how to prepare.

You will want to know everything possible about the multiple-choice exams you are scheduled to take. Ask your teaching staff for information about the types of questions which you can expect. It's perfectly reasonable to ask about: the numbers of questions in the examination; the different types of questions (problem solving, definitions, case studies, theory-based, etc.) ; any differential weightings for the various sections of the exam;

and, of course date, venue and the starting and finishing times of the exam. If you find that multiple-choice questions will be a prominent part of the exam, then a considerable part of your preparation should be geared specifically for this form of question.

Preparing for multiple-choice questions

Martina enrolled in a science course with the intention of majoring in psychology. She enjoyed the lectures and prepared for her mid-term exams as she had done in high school, by writing summaries of her class notes. She went over these summaries many times and walked into the exam full of confidence. Martina was shocked when she found that she had failed the multiple-choice part of the exam.

Her tutor referred her for counselling and in the referral note, she mentioned that Martina needed to improve her examination skills, specifically her preparation for multiple-choice tests. During the first counselling session, Martina was surprised to find that studying summaries is generally not a recommended preparation for multiple-choice exams. Why? Because summaries are too broad in scope and multiple-choice questions (MCQ) can be very specific. The details which you would not consider including in your summary could well be the focus of MCQs.

The best preparation for multiple-choice exams is to read over your *refined* notes—your class notes which have been supplemented with additions, corrections and side flaps (see the chapter on note-taking for more information). Repeated readings of your notes will help to fix the broad themes and specific details in your mind. You may be wondering how many times you should go through your notes before a multiple-choice exam. Basically, it depends on your understanding of the concepts dealt with in the lectures, but for most students, five times would be a reasonable target. In order to help you prepare more thoroughly for these difficult examinations, here are some practical pointers to apply.

Practical pointers for answering multiple-choice questions

- Be certain to correctly fill in the identification block.

- Check that the answer space number corresponds to the question number.
- Do all of the easy questions first; return to the more difficult ones for reconsideration.
- When reading the questions, underline the key terms to focus your attention on the specific issue(s) being questioned. Make marginal notes on the question sheet if that helps you to clarify your thinking.
- Be careful in your interpretation of critical words such as many, some, none, always, sometimes, never, more, less, best and least. These words give specific meanings to the question content.
- Make certain your answer marks fully fill the answer space and do not make stray marks on the answer sheet. The optical scanning equipment might misread these marks as answers.
- If you have been told that there is no penalty for guessing, then be certain that one answer is recorded for *every* question. If, on the other hand, guessing is penalised, then record an answer if you can narrow the choices down to two possibilities.
- When trying to choose between two remaining options out of the five, ask yourself how would your lecturer answer this question. Putting yourself in the shoes of a knowledgeable person should help you to make a more informed decision.
- As you work your way through the examination, make a mark on the question sheet of the items you would like to reconsider, if time is available at the end.
- Do not change an answer unless you know that the recorded answer is definitely wrong. Studies have shown that your first answer is more likely to be correct, barring the situation where new information comes to light.
- Cheating is definitely not advised. Many nationally administered exams have built in devices which can detect similarities in answering patterns amongst the candidates. Additionally, some examinations have several different formats such that the questions are arranged in different locations on the question sheets.

When you receive your results, you will probably not be given a copy of the questions. Good multiple-choice questions take considerable effort to develop and once done, the examiners like to keep them for possible use in later years. However, if you have specific questions, you may be able to see your lecturer individually and go over certain questions. Given that your exam marks contribute very substantially to your overall result, it is best to make use of every possible learning opportunity. For local examinations, your teaching staff may be willing to go over the exam questions and your answers with you.

Short answer questions

Of all the possible types of exam questions, some of the most predictable are those requiring you to write just a sentence or perhaps one paragraph. These questions will frequently ask you to define critical terms or give some interpretation. The best way to prepare is to make a list of important definitions and then to learn them. Consider using flash cards with the term written on one side and the definition written on the other. Prepare these cards following each lecture as you progress through the semester and learn the terms during waiting periods each day.

When answering short answer questions, be certain to be concise—hence the name. Get right to the point; don't waffle. If necessary, use bullet points to cover any details which you believe to be essential to your answer.

Essay questions

The most common type of exam question is the essay. This type of question is designed to test your knowledge of the concepts and to assess your ability to write logically and concisely. In order to succeed in essay questions, apply the following practical pointers to improve your responses.

Be sure to read the question *carefully*. Underline the topic terms (the words dealing with the concept(s) which are the focus of the question) in red ink and the operative terms in blue. The latter terms tell you what operations you are to carry out, such as describe, critically analyse, trace the development of, evaluate, justify, etc. If you are unclear about how these terms differ, refer to pages 106–107 in *How To Pass Exams*, the companion volume to this book.

Jot down any initial ideas. Even while reading the question, if you have an idea, write it down straightaway. Some of these initial ideas could well be helpful in triggering further thoughts or in helping to structure your essay. If they are not written down, they could be lost, a cause of considerable frustration.

Having read the question and underlined the terms as suggested above, organise your ideas using an outline approach. You might start with the structural headings: introduction, body and conclusion. Under each of these headings, write any topical ideas which you think are relevant. As part of your mark will be based upon how well you organise and then develop your ideas, it is important for you to understand very clearly the functions of your essay sections.

The introduction to the essay

The introduction is strategically a very important section as it will establish a set of either positive or negative expectations in the mind of the marker. Place yourself in the marker's role. What is foremost in your mind as you start to read yet another exam essay? The prime concern for the marker is to determine where on the marking scale the writer of the present essay seems to be located. Your job is to start off very strongly so the marker is thinking, 'Yes, this *is* good—clear, logical, and well organised!'

If the introduction is written well, you are off to a good start. If it is handled poorly, then the marker's impression of your work will probably be a negative one. Thus, make your introduction clear, concise and spot on target. If you are fogbound and befuddled about the question, try using what I call the TIM approach. This is an acronym standing for *topic, importance* and *method*—three functions you can carry out in the introductory paragraph(s) to get off to a positive start. The first task is to state what the topic is about. Choose the topic terms which you underlined in the question and define them. Having defined the terms, then state why they are important. The assumption is that the essay questions on a major exam will focus upon important issues in the course. Finally, tell the marker how you will be dealing with, or structuring your response.

Remember to make the job easy for the marker. Marking many, many essays is no fun; in fact it's a lot of very hard work. If the marker picks up the final essay (yours!) at 1.00 am after a very long and tiring evening and reads a first paragraph of rubbish, then your essay is in trouble. You're in even more trouble if your handwriting is indecipherable!

The marker wants clarity and certainty, just like the traveller who is seeking directions in a foreign country. If you provide a clear set of instructions with signposts to look for on the way, the traveller will feel more relaxed and confident. The marker is taking a journey through your essay. Tell the marker how your essay is organised and structured. Then specify the parts to look for during the reading process. Here is a sample question and an introductory paragraph using the TIM approach.

Question: Compare the economic theories of Marx and Keynes with reference to the national economic situation over the past two years.

TIM introduction: 'The writings of two economic philosophers, Marx and Keynes, have continued to have an impact upon current economic conditions. This essay will firstly present a brief synopsis of Marxist and Keynesian theories and then discuss how each theory relates to three national economic situations which have strongly influenced this country over the past two years: inflation, unemployment and the national trade balance.'

Having read this introductory paragraph, the marker should feel confident and comfortable about the essay. That is, a positive set of expectations has been established and gives every indication of being fulfilled as the marker progresses to the body of the essay.

Body

Any exam essay is going to be time limited. You will have only a short time to write, so try to organise the body so that no more than three major ideas are dealt with. For convenience, you might apply the Rule of 3. That is, try to generate three ideas or concepts which are logically related to each other and, very importantly, to the central focus of the question.

In the example above, having defined the theories of Marx and Keynes, each of these theories was then to be applied to three economic situations: inflation, unemployment and the national trade balance. Structurally, the body might look like this:

Definitions
    Marxist theory
    Keynesian theory
Applications
    Inflation
        Marxist interpretation
        Keynesian interpretation
    Unemployment
        Marxist interpretation
        Keynesian interpretation
    National trade balance
        Marxist interpretation
        Keynesian interpretation

In actual practice, you would not use the headings, definitions and applications, but would move smoothly from paragraph to paragraph and from section to section with appropriately worded transitions. For example, having discussed the inflationary aspects in terms of Marxist and Keynesian theories, you might say something like, 'Having dealt with inflation, the first of the three economic situations, I would now like to turn to unemployment and compare the implications of Marxist and Keynesian theories.' The marker will know exactly where you are in the essay and where you are heading. Once again, deal with the topics in an organised and logically developed pattern and make the marker's job easy. You may want to check with your teaching staff to see whether preference is given to the use of either first or third person in your responses.

Conclusion

Aside from creating positive expectations during the introduction and guiding the marker step by step through the body, it is very important to leave the reader with a positive impression of your work at the end. The conclusion should wrap up the essential features of your logically constructed argument and move on to a statement of what you conclude. You might want to return to the initial question and draw from it the wording of the key terms, so that the conclusion actually reflects the essence of the question.

Using the traveller's analogy, we tend to feel more comfortable with others who speak our own language. In the exam conclusion, you want to establish maximum confidence and comfort in the examiner just before the mark is written on your paper. Seeing the key terms of the question applied to logically developed conclusions will certainly go a long way towards winning you high marks on your essays.

Before leaving this section, it is important to mention that writing good examination essays is a challenging and difficult skill and will require considerable practice. Ask your teaching staff if you could write several sample essays under time-limited conditions and have them give you their quick impressions of your responses. Practice and relevant feedback will hasten the development of your skills.

Checking your essay

Let's say that your essay has been rigorously and rationally structured and argued and you have drawn pertinent and logical conclusions. However, the marker has had to tolerate in your essay many careless errors, mostly in the form of misspellings and minor grammatical mistakes. What impact are these errors likely to have upon your mark? Disaster. Most markers will be frustrated by these errors and they may jump to some negative conclusions: students who can't spell correctly or who can't write grammatically correct English don't deserve to pass! Be certain that you run over your essay quickly and correct any errors in spelling and grammar so that your mark reflects the quality of your thinking, not the carelessness of hasty writing.

Open-book exams

Dennis, an accountancy graduate, was enrolled for his professional year, a particularly difficult training experience which qualifies successful candidates for certification as chartered accountants. Aside from the difficulties of working full-time and studying part-time, Dennis and his colleagues had to pass the periodic exams, all of which were open-book exams.

Dennis initially thought open-book exams were gifts from heaven. As he was preparing for his first set of exams, he consoled himself when he came to a particularly difficult part in the syllabus, saying, 'If that appears on the exam, I can always look it up.' However, he was unaware of how often he said this to himself. When exam day arrived, he entered the room with a load of books which would have threatened the integrity of your average supermarket trolley. He started the exam paper and quickly found that he was having to check, read, search, consolidate and deduce all too often. He simply did not know his notes and his reference materials well enough. Those exams were a total failure, but he learned from the experience. He was much more adequately prepared for the next exams and progressed without further setbacks through the examination series to the completion of his certification.

If you are enrolled in subjects which have open-book exams, be aware of the following points.

- Beware: open-book exams can engender a false sense of security. Having your reference books immediately available is not the recipe for instant exam success.
- Prepare as you would for a normal exam, but mark critical pages in your reference sources with Post-It notes and relevant labels for quick checking.
- Examiners may expect higher quality responses in open-book exams because of the availability of your reference materials.

Laboratory exams

As a veteran of many science-based studies, I can recall in vivid detail the anxiety associated with lab exams. Following an intense preparation period of staring down microscopes, hunching over lab tables, and probing specimen after specimen, we were invited into the laboratory on exam day to test our recognition and recall by playing what we cynically called 'musical microscopes'. We progressed from one station to the next when the alarm sounded and then inspected the tagged item and answered any related questions.

Lab exams require extremely thorough preparation. Over the weeks preceding the exam, be certain to revise the samples and materials very well. For example, in subjects like histology, the microscopic study of tissues and cells, be certain to look at many different slides of the same type of tissue, as there can be a wide range of normal variations. Reviewing just your own set of slides is a decided gamble—move around amongst your colleagues and look at their specimens as well. Note particularly any differences in texture, colour, stain intensity, and especially the surrounding tissues which might give clues to the identity of the central material.

Help each other by setting up practice exams and quizzing each other. Whether your lab exam is in histology or physics, the same principles apply. Variety of exposure and thoroughness in preparation are the keys to success. Here are a few additional practical pointers.

- Prepare week by week for lab exams. Don't gamble on the lab being open the day or two before the exam, as the staff might need this time to set up the required equipment and displays.
- High powers of concentration will be necessary—be certain to get adequate rest leading up to the exam.
- If you wear glasses, clean the lenses prior to the exam. No sense looking at intricate material through foggy lenses.
- During the exam, should you skip a space on the answer sheet, be very careful that your next responses are placed in the correct spaces.
- If you think that a display has been disturbed or the pointer on a microscope is incorrectly positioned, summon a proctor immediately.
- Given the intensity and difficulty of most lab exams, at the conclusion of each 'ordeal', discuss with classmates how you could improve your preparation for the next one. Share thoughts and resources with your colleagues.

Auditions in the performing arts

Auditions are critical examinations in that the outcome frequently determines whether the candidate gains admission to a training program or, even more critically, whether the candidate obtains a job. The practical pointers listed below were developed in conjunction with the National Institute of Dramatic Arts (NIDA), Sydney, Australia, where handling auditions well is the key to admission and ultimately jobs.

- Contact the theatre, agency, school or institution for whom you intend to audition to obtain as early as possible the relevant details (date, time and place of the auditions and the work(s) to be prepared).
- Try to establish who will be auditioning you. What is their background? What are their likes and dislikes? Any information about the judges will help you in your preparation.
- If time permits, talk to friends and colleagues who are established in the relevant field and ask for their advice on your work and audition material.
- Visit the place where your audition is to be held so that you are familiar with the surroundings and any problems posed by the space (for example, a small stage, background noise, poor lighting). Try to accommodate these limitations when rehearsing for your audition.
- Prepare and practise your audition material *very* thoroughly. The more prepared you are, the more relaxed and confident you are likely to be.
- Prior to the audition day, perform your work in front of several knowledgeable friends and experienced colleagues. Ask for detailed and constructive criticism on your performance.
- Make any adjustments to your performance which you think are justified on the basis of the feedback from your friends and colleagues.
- Following your intensive and thorough preparation period, get a good night's rest before the day of the audition. However, expect that you may toss and turn quite a bit the night before. If you have always been very nervous under these circumstances, then read and practise the relaxation training procedure described in Chapter 9.

- Arrive sufficiently early before your audition so that you have plenty of warming-up time. Doing some vigorous exercises can help loosen your body and release nervous tension.
- Don't make unjust comparisons between yourself and the performers who precede you. Think positively. Close your eyes and see yourself performing well. Say repeatedly to yourself, '*I can do it!!*'
- If you get too nervous, close your eyes and picture a large stop sign. Say 'Stop!' to yourself and then say 'Relax-x-x-x-x'.
- When called to perform, pause briefly and say to yourself, 'I can do it!'. Take a comfortable breath and then rise to the occasion, and *do it*!
- In some auditions, you may be stopped midway through your performance. The comments offered during the interruption might be tactful, but they could also be abrasive. Accept the remarks objectively and do not take any criticism personally.
- If you are unsuccessful in your audition, contact the auditioning authority or agency a few days later. Ask for feedback, specifically, how you could improve your performance and/or auditioning skills.

The medical viva examination

The medical viva exam is a particularly difficult assessment used to evaluate the clinical and communication skills of undergraduate and post-graduate candidates. Generally, the candidate is asked to examine a patient and then report the clinical findings and answer questions from two examining clinicians. The following notes have been obtained from questionnaires and interviews completed by individuals examined in the teaching hospitals of the University of New South Wales, Sydney, Australia.

- Allow for considerable preparation time and organise many practice vivas with hospital staff or more senior colleagues.
- Practise quick and logical thinking by volunteering to speak during ward rounds.

- During the examination, do not assume that the absence of any feedback from the examiners means that you are doing poorly. The examiners are often instructed to be 'poker-faced' and to offer no feedback.
- Try to elaborate on your answers with relevant supporting information. You are in control over the examination while you are speaking relevantly and constructively about the topic under question.
- When asked for your opinion or diagnosis, practise the Rule of 3. Give three possible diagnoses, A, B and C and then rank them in order of priority. Even if the correct diagnosis is B and you have nominated A or C, you still have mentioned B and possibly some logical means by which you have discounted it.
- Do not fabricate tests and procedures if you can not justify their use.
- If asked a question and you are stumped, request a restatement of the question or clarification to obtain more thinking time.
- If, after further thinking, you can come up with nothing, say you don't know and ask if you can move on to another question.
- If aggressive or confronting examiners are a problem for you, practise with staff or colleagues who can take on this role. Practise being cool under fire.
- Know the established and set routines for examining the different parts of the patient.
- Learn the relevant questions, data and procedures associated with the important disease states in a systems approach so that one fact suggests the next.
- If you feel you know your theoretical material but get too nervous in the viva situation to represent your knowledge well, then consult a psychologist experienced in examination performance skills. Well prepared but nervous candidates can improve their exam marks by up to 30 per cent by reducing their anxiety.
- In order to get a handle on the range of cases which might be presented, make the assumption that you will be asked to examine patients with reasonably common disorders. Categorise the range of possible cases under trauma, infection, neoplasm, congenital and infarction. List the five

most common clinical situations under each of these headings and then know everything about these 25 entities. That helps to narrow the scope of your intensive learning.

- During the exam, pause briefly after the question is asked. You are in control during this silent time. Too rapid an answer robs you of time to organise your answer.

- If you realise that you have given an erroneous response, say so straightaway and ask if you can offer a more considered answer.

- When absolutely stuck and you feel you can not pass directly on to yet another question, start your response in general terms, perhaps by rephrasing some parts of the question and then move onto more specific details. Sometimes the momentum can get you moving onto areas where you are more knowledgeable.

- Some students get thrown off guard when they are asked a question which they think is too easy. Go ahead and answer it, as it is stated.

- Think positively about the viva exam. To have progressed to your current position means that you can handle thinking under pressure. Give yourself credit for your strengths and prior accomplishments.

- Work with a small group of candidates and video film your practice sessions. Pay particular attention to your body language. Do you look confident? If not, why not? Ask some experienced colleagues how you can develop a more confident approach.

- Some candidates believe that vivas test professional small talk and theatrical abilities as much as theoretical considerations. They are probably overestimating the role of the small talk, but being able to offer these fillers between the facts can keep the examiners at bay. Practise keeping the communication process moving and oriented in a positive direction even when your knowledge of the basic issue is somewhat thin.

- Do not expect to answer every question in the viva. Sometimes examiners will throw in a very difficult question to distinguish between a distinction and high distinction performance.

- Worrying will not win you marks in vivas. Rather than

worry about your forthcoming performance, replace any apprehension with a positive, firm statement: *I can do it!!*

Practical exercises

Performing well in examinations is mostly a function of knowing your material very well. However, there is also the element of being able to perform under pressure. Here are some exercises which you might practise in order to help you perform to your highest potential.

1 Prepare mini essays

Practise thinking and writing quickly by composing a one-page mini essay on one of the items on the TV evening news. Have the mini essay completed before the finish of the news broadcast. Give your response to a family member or flatmate for feedback.

2 Practise the TIM approach for exam essays

Practise writing the introductory paragraph to each of the essays found on past exam papers. If past papers are not available, then ask a colleague to make up a list of sample exam essays. Remember to tell the reader how your essay is structured to make the marking process as easy as possible.

3 Practise quick thinking

If you believe your mind is just not quick enough, practise getting it moving more quickly. Play games such as theatre sports and charades. Ask a colleague to list five speaking topics such as, my most embarrassing experience; the place I would most like to visit; the most memorable teacher I have had. These topics relate to your own experiences and should be less threatening than theoretical subjects. The rules of the exercise are: no preparation time—just start talking and do so for at least one minute. The topics can be increased in difficulty as you improve your skills at spontaneous thinking and appropriate delivery.

11
Responding effectively in exams

- The day and night before the exams
- Morning strategies on exam day
- Arriving at the venue
- Reading the instructions correctly
- Resting between questions
- Dealing with mental blocks
- Keeping panic at bay
- Checking your work
- Practical exercises

Beverley, a second-year technical college student in a travel and tourism certificate course, had performed very well on her assignments through the year. However, she had put off her serious revision until the one week 'stu vac' just prior to her yearly exams. She had a mountain of work to revise and only 168 hours available (that's seven days at 24 hours each). Is that sufficient time to cover the year's work? Most experienced students would say, 'No'.

Beverley was in a panic during that last week. She rushed through her notes, crammed information, lived on fast food, drank too much coffee and got far too little sleep. By Day One of the exam period, she was a nervous wreck. By Day Three, she was worse, as evidenced by her sleeping through her alarm and arriving half an hour late for her nine o'clock exam. As you might guess, the exams were a disaster.

It is to be hoped that your examination experiences are quite different from Beverley's. Even though you might have performed quite well during the academic year, you will want to continue your winning performance during the critical final exams. If you have followed the advice emphasised in this book, you will have prepared each week from the very beginning of the year for your final exams. Even with this thorough prepara-tion, there are still some exam week pitfalls which you will want to consider.

The day and night before the exams

Let's assume that you have been preparing steadily through the year. It's now the day before your first exam. What's likely to be going through your head? Very probably you will be thinking whether you will pass and pass well. There is always that lingering doubt that your study materials have not been covered well enough.

In order to deal with these niggling doubts, put an end to them with a firm, positive statement: '*I can do it!!*' (meaning that you can perform well on the exams). In the exam context, you will certainly be thinking prior to these important events, so you might as well be thinking positive thoughts.

In those final hours before the exams, browse through your notes and run through the general issues in your mind. It's not the time to challenge your mind with new and difficult concepts.

Should you discover a chapter or article which you have forgotten and which you think is very examinable, then *calmly* decide how you can glean its significance in a short time. Speed read the chapter and look specifically for the most examinable points.

Even though you will probably be quite anxious, try to get to bed early enough so you can get a reasonable night's sleep. But, if you're a heavy sleeper, set two alarms with one on the far side of the room. You might place the second alarm next to a bucket of water so that you can splash cold water on your face once you've reached the alarm.

Getting to sleep the night before exams

To get your mind off the exam and into a more relaxed state, focus on your breathing and, after a few comfortably deep breaths, start counting backwards from 100 when you breathe in. See the number being drawn in your mind, say it to yourself, and trace the number with a finger tip in the palm of the opposite hand. With those sensory inputs preoccupying your mind, you will not have the opportunity to think of anything else, including the exam. By counting tenaciously from 100 backwards, you will bore yourself off to sleep.

The morning of the exam

If you want to put a final polishing on your understanding of the central concepts, then rise early and go through the notes one more time. Just page through the notes and focus upon the major headings. Don't let your mind break away and think catastrophic thoughts, for example, about being confronted with an impossible question. As stated above, displace any negative thoughts with a firm and positive, '*I can do it!!*' Before leaving for the exam, check to see that you have all requisite equipment for the particular exam: student ID, pens, ruler, calculator (if allowed) and any other special equipment required for the subject.

Murphy's Law states that if anything is ever going to go wrong, it will happen at the most inappropriate time. Murphy must have based the law upon exam candidates, as it's uncanny how often they experience quite extraordinary events just before exams. Illness is very common, but the list can also include relationship breakdowns, theft of class notes, death of loved ones, car theft, public transport failures, and even physical assault on the way to the exam. One forgetful student who took nine years to complete a three-year degree, requested special consideration following the deaths of his maternal grandmother. According to his reports, she died on two occasions, just before the final exams in his second and seventh years of his degree. The administration was not sympathetic on the second occasion. By the way, if untoward events do occur, be sure to obtain documentation from a relevant authority, such as a doctor, lawyer, or police officer.

To cater for delays and disruptions which can certainly occur on exam days, be certain to get an early start after you have had a good breakfast. Some students claim they don't need breakfast, but the research evidence shows a strong positive correlation between concentration powers and adequate nutrition. Thinking very actively for three consecutive hours is hard work and work requires energy. Relying upon last evening's fuel to sustain your mental fire in an exam the following morning could well result in a cold performance.

Arriving at the venue

Careful students will confirm the date, time and venue of their exams prior to the examination period. You will certainly receive no marks for arriving at the venue 24 hours late. Assuming that you are arriving on time, when you get to the venue, avoid the doom and gloom squad. There are always some students who take responsibility on these occasions for spreading chaos and confusion. Avoid individuals who are likely to dash up to you and ask for your opinion about an unknown author of an obscure article which they claim is central to the exam. Simply locate yourself in a quiet corner away from the crowd and run through your major headings once again.

When you are asked to enter the exam room, consider carefully the choice of seat, if you are allowed to make a choice.

Take into consideration whether you will bake in strong sunlight, freeze in a cold draught, or be disturbed by a colleague who is renowned for cracking knuckles or coughing frequently. I found sitting in front was generally best, as the only distraction might be talkative proctors, but you can always politely ask them to speak more quietly, if they must speak at all.

Reading the instructions

Most students at some stage have misread critical instructions. I did in a philosophy exam. Having been accustomed to writing two or three essays in a three-hour exam, I raced ahead and chose two of the three options and then moved on to the short answer part of the exam. I found the exam to be very long, but just managed to finish in time. At the doorstep, a group of classmates asked which essay I had selected. I said the first and third. My response was met with quizzical expressions. One classmate exclaimed that we were only required to do *one* essay. That frantic 30 minutes spent writing the superfluous essay was wasted. But, I did learn a very valuable lesson.

In order to avoid making a similar mistake, read the instructions *twice* and the second time through, *underline the operative words*. By taking these careful steps, you should have fixed firmly in your mind what exactly is required.

Resting between questions

As mentioned above, concentrating on an examination paper for three consecutive hours is a tiring task. Even if you've managed to get a reasonable amount of sleep the night before and you've had a good breakfast, your mind will still tire during the exam. One way to help maintain your concentration is to take frequent, but short breaks during the actual exam.

After finishing the first section of the exam, put your pen down, close your eyes, let your body relax, and then focus on your breathing. As you breathe slowly in and out over the next three breaths, say to yourself, 'Relax'. Then quietly extend your arms and legs. Return to the exam and read the instructions for the next section or question *twice*.

Taking periodic brief rests will help you to stay fresh, both mentally and physically. Your powers of concentration, your ability to recall material, and your creativity in composing essays will all benefit from the short rest breaks taken four to six times during long exams.

Dealing with mental blocks

Occasionally the unthinkable (taken literally) will happen. You are progressing reasonably well with the exam and turn the page to read the next question. No sooner do your eyes focus on the key terms of the question, than your mind shuts down, full stop. As you fight to regain your grip on the topic, panic begins to rise. Your mind has no difficulty focusing upon thoughts of impending failure, which only makes the matter worse. What can you do under these circumstances?

Firstly, practise the brief relaxation exercise described above. Close your eyes, relax shoulders and jaws, take three slow and comfortable breaths and say, 'Relax. I can do it!' Having displaced the panic and taken some of the rigidity out of your system, then draw a rectangle on some scrap paper or in the margin of the exam paper. Write the key topics of the question in the centre of the rectangle and then try to write four associated ideas, terms, correlates or whatever, one at each of the corners. Having written three or four of these terms, then try to put some relevant ideas on the sides of the rectangle. Can you draw arrows connecting any two or more ideas?

Having constructed this idea rectangle, you will probably find that something relevant will come to mind. The goal of the exercise is to relax and then let your mind deal with associates of the key ideas. Any lever which you can use to loosen the gears of the mind is worth trying. As stated before, relevant words in the essay space will always be worth more than a gaping blank space.

Keeping panic at bay

In spite of thorough preparation and positive precautions, you might still experience a panic attack. That fleeting negative thought about failure can spark a conflagration of physical and emotional chaos. Your heart pounds, your breathing accelerates, your limbs shake, your brow sweats and your mind whirls— hardly the conditions for writing essays or answering mind-probing multiple-choice questions. What can you do if you experience a panic attack in an exam?

You've read about the process before in this book, but it is worth repeating. Close your eyes and focus on your breathing. You want to slow your breathing rate down because rapid, shallow breathing can promote further panic responses. In order to regain mental control and calmness, count backwards slowly from ten to zero, pairing each number with an exhalation. To increase your concentration, you might try 10 000 and ten, 9 000 and nine, 8 000 and eight, and so on to 1 000 and one, zero thousand and zero. That number sequence will keep your mind fixed on a non-arousing series, thus allowing your body responses to return to a more calm state.

At the end of the counting sequence, say to yourself, '*I can manage this exam!*' several times. Open your eyes and proceed to the next question.

If the panic responses return, then consider asking a proctor if you can be excused to go to the lavatory. Having moved from the exam room to the lavatory, splash cold water on your face, take a couple of comfortable breaths and say, 'Relax', as you breathe out. Then, having settled yourself, return to the exam room and try to get on with the exam paper.

If these measures fail, then tell the proctor that you can not proceed with the exam and excuse yourself. Go directly to a doctor or counsellor and discuss the reactions you experienced in the exam. You will need to obtain a certificate to document your visit and the difficulties you experienced in the exam. Write to the registrar or other relevant exam authority and explain what happened. Ask for information about alternative assessment procedures. It might be helpful also to see the coordinator for the subject and submit a copy of the documentation. The coordinator might be able to give you details about a possible deferred examination.

In summary, examinations are stressful and students can experience a wide range of reactions just before and during these important events. Prepare well before your exams and

know as much as possible about the exam content and procedures. A prepared mind copes much better, especially under
stressful circumstances.

Check your paper

If you finish your examination with some time to spare, resist
the temptation to leave immediately. You can use the remainder
of the time to look over your paper. Check to see that you have
recorded correctly your name, student number and any other
requested details. Look over your essays and correct any misspellings or grammatical errors. Finally, reconsider any
multiple-choice items which you may have passed over initially.
It is often the case that later questions prompt recall of information which will allow you to attempt more successfully an
earlier question. Finally, make sure that there are no random
marks on your multiple-choice answer sheet, if one is used on
your exam.

Practical exercises

1 Anticipate multiple-choice exam questions

Form a syndicate of three or four classmates and delegate sections of the class notes to each one. The goal is for the students
to revise their delegated section and to write three questions
which they believe to be the three most examinable issues from
each lecture. Each student in the syndicate photocopies their
questions and outlined responses and gives a copy to the other
members. If possible, meet to discuss the questions and nominated answers.

2 Write your own essay questions

Essay questions are generally designed to test your knowledge of
broader issues. Often you may be given five essay questions
from which you are to select three for answering. In order to
anticipate possible questions, look over your syllabus and note
the prominent concepts. Ask yourself, 'If I were the examiner,
what five questions could I develop which would cover the

major issues dealt with in the course?'. Of course, you can gain a wider perspective by working in a syndicate and having the members each develop five questions and then prepare a one-page outline of an 'ideal' response. Photocopy the outlines and then meet to discuss the strengths and weaknesses.

3 Examine past papers

If past papers are available to you, go over the exam questions from the last five years. Note any trends or similarities in question topics. If the same general issue has been the focus of two or three questions over the past five years, then emphasise that topic area in your revision.

4 Mind control . . . peak performance

As suggested in several chapters of this book, gaining maximal control over your mind's activities can benefit you in your exams. If worries and lapses in concentration are problems, start straightaway with the relaxation training procedure described in Chapter 9. The relaxation training will help you to cope with nervousness before and during exams. It will also increase your powers of concentration. Twice daily practice for about three months will be needed to obtain a strong relaxation response. With that conditioned response available, even the most frightening exam question can be viewed with competence, confidence and control.